THE BASIC ARTS OF MANAGEMENT

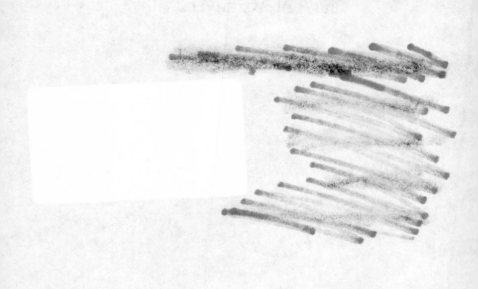

W. J. TAYLOR
AND T. F. WATLING

THE BASIC
ARTS OF
MANAGEMENT

Second Edition

BUSINESS BOOKS

London   Melbourne   Sydney   Auckland   Johannesburg

Business Books Ltd
An imprint of the Hutchinson Publishing Group
17–21 Conway Street, London W1P 6JD

Hutchinson Publishing Group (Australia) Pty Ltd
16–22 Church Street, Hawthorn, Melbourne, Victoria 3122

Hutchinson Group (NZ) Ltd
32–34 View Road, PO Box 40–086, Glenfield, Auckland 10

Hutchinson Group (SA) (Pty) Ltd
PO Box 337, Bergvlei 2012, South Africa

First published 1972
Second Edition 1985

Set in Times New Roman by Folio Photosetting, Bristol

Printed and bound in England by
Anchor Brendon Ltd, Tiptree, Essex

British Library Cataloguing in Publication Data
Taylor, W.
    The basic arts of management.
    1. Management
    I. Title II. Watling, T.F.
    658   HD31

Library of Congress Cataloging in Publication Data
Taylor, W.J. (William John)
    The basic arts of management.
    Bibliography: p.
    Includes index
    1. Management. I. Watling, Thomas Francis. II. Title.
    HD31.T33 1985 658   85–3842

ISBN   0 09 160781 7

By the same authors:
Successful Project Management
Practical Project Management

Contents

Acknowledgements

We thank Steven Trigg ACMA for his helpful comments and our wives for their patience and forbearance.

We are grateful to ICL for permission to publish. However, the views expressed are our own and not necessarily those of ICL.

Introduction

The Basic Arts of Management was first published in 1972, but there has been a great deal of change since then, particularly in the environment of the modern manager. We have therefore revised much of the text for this new edition. We believe that, like the original, it will provide a sound introduction to the arts of management for the student and younger manager and a useful restatement for the older manager. Much of the content is applicable to business owners and the self-employed.

The struggle to compete and improve productivity has created an even tougher environment for management. This has led to greater concern with marketing and has sharpened awareness of the need for effective management of people and money. Advances in information technology (IT) are changing the pace and style of management life; and organizations and operational methods.

We open the book with a look at the information technology revolution and the environment within which the manager of today and tomorrow will have to operate. Next we look at the important matter of managing yourself. It is a truism that you cannot manage other people effectively until you have learned to manage yourself.

A manager, by definition, obtains results through the people he or she manages. Effective management of people brings results. The manager needs to understand:

- What makes people perform well
- The opportunities which responsibility for people brings
- The mechanics of people management

Regrettably, today's manager also has to be familiar with the three Rs of the modern world – redeployment, redundancy and retirement – because he may have to manage situations involving them. From a more immediate and personal aspect, he may be on the receiving end.

People are a manager's key resource but results are measured in money. Organizations – and the jobs of managers in those organizations – do not survive unless they offer good value for money. In the private sector, organizations have to make a profit. In the public sector organizations have to show a target return on the resources entrusted to them. We start our consideration of money by looking at accountancy in management. From there we go on to consider money and its place in the manager's job:

- Budgeting
- Performance against budget
- Evaluation of investment opportunities

Managers have always been concerned with information. Other things being equal, the manager who has the best information, and knows how to use it, wins. The advances in information technology can give the manager more and better information, and the opportunities start on your own desk. We consider some techniques for using and interpreting information in forecasting, planning and progressing.

Every silver lining has its cloud and information technology has brought concern over data security, data protection and data privacy. We take a brief overview of these concerns and how they affect the manager.

We conclude *The Basic Arts of Management* with the seven keys to a successful career in management.

Throughout the book we have used the term 'he', although we hasten to add that many managers and entrepreneurs are women. Hence 'he' should be interpreted as 'he' or 'she'.

PART 1

Managing in the information technology world

1 The Information Technology (IT) Revolution

The information age

Information technology or IT is the key factor shaping our working environment. IT will impact on the way of life of everyone in the developed world. It will penetrate every aspect of life from the cradle to the grave. The manager will not escape its impact.

Powerful forces are leading us into the information age. Advancing computer technology brings more power at lower prices. Telecommunications and office products are becoming more flexible, easier, and more economic to use. Computers are linked into networks by telecommunications. British Telecom's exchanges and handsets incorporate computers. Office products are increasingly controlled or replaced by computer technology. The word processor is replacing the typewriter. Telecommunications, computing, and office products are converging into the irresistible force behind the IT revolution. IT is the key to increasing productivity in the office.

The need to understand IT

It is vital for managers to understand IT and how it may affect their firms and their jobs, so that they recognize the opportunities that IT offers. IT will change the management environment out of recognition. In the process it will eliminate the jobs of many managers and, no doubt, will create new ones. New managers may adapt to the changes relatively easily and learn the necessary new skills, though they may also find that there are fewer managerial jobs to compete for. Older managers may find the changes more difficult. If they do not meet the challenge, a different challenge may be forced upon them by redundancy.

It's not just computers

IT is more than just the introduction of computers. Most large organizations already have their data processing (DP) departments with mainframe computers. Micros, personal computers, and terminals are to be seen in organizations of every size right down to the one man business. IT brings together all aspects of information handling. In particular, it is the marriage of conventional computing with telecommunications. IT will also substitute for many conventional office facilities like filing cabinets, wall charts, and diaries.

There have been forecasts of the paperless office, of integrated management information systems, and of the computer revolution, for so long that managers can be forgiven for being a bit sceptical. They look at the queue outside the DP manager's door waiting for the development of new systems. They see how long it takes to develop a new system or to change an existing one. This reflects the fact that DP departments have for years brought about massive productivity improvements in every department but their own. Computer manufacturers have improved the price performance of computing equipment out of all recognition since LEO 1 performed the first commercial computing task in the world for the bakery of J. Lyons & Co. in 1954. In the early fifties a computer cost a million pounds or more and was probably made to order for the buyer. It occupied a specially fitted and air-conditioned room the size of a tennis court. Its operators were highly skilled and were, more often than not, graduates. The machines broke down often and were of limited capacity. Today you can buy for less than £5000 a more powerful computer, which has a larger memory, is more reliable, and can be operated by an intelligent clerk after a couple of days training. Compared with this, the productivity of systems design and programming departments has improved only marginally over the last thirty years.

Price performance improvements in hardware will certainly continue at a dramatic pace for the rest of this century as a result of developments in chip technology already under way. The raw power and capacity will be there at an ever dwindling price and the end users and potential end users of that power and capacity are determined to get their hands on it one way or another. In some cases they will just bypass the DP department and buy their own micros or personal computers. In others, DP managers are seeking ways to develop new systems more rapidly, as well as ways to allow users to develop their own programs on the company network. There is now much greater willingness to use standard package programs and a vast software industry has grown up to supply them. There is also great interest in techniques and tools for the development of programs tailored to the user's needs.

In the early days of computing, hardware was expensive and software relatively cheap. Today the position is reversed. Hardware costs are dropping by around 90 per cent every seven years. Software costs, largely labour costs, are still rising rapidly. In consequence, more intelligence is being built into the hardware. One of the more interesting hardware developments of recent years is the Content Addressable File Store (CAFS). This allows a user to search large backing stores very rapidly and is said to reduce from pounds to pence the cost of making a computer enquiry or search.

When computers were priced in tens or hundreds of thousands of pounds, they had to be kept fully loaded and hard at work. In the early 1960s it was common for programmers to wait for three or four days for computer time to test their programs. Now the situation is different. People costs are high. Capital and running costs for a computer are low and falling rapidly. It is already common for programmers to have immediate access to a powerful computer through their desk-top terminal. Similarly, other users who need instant information have immediate access to their computer-held databases. In the not so distant future, powerful, intelligent computer terminals will sit on the desk of every office worker – managers included. They will not be concerned that the terminal is used for only a few minutes a day. They will be treated as telephones are today – there for the convenience of the users.

User convenience

Indeed the convenience of the user is the keynote of the thinking and development in the IT industry today. IT is a highly competitive international business with some giant firms and many thousands of smaller ones. Those firms that survive appreciate the second message of the business environment. The customer is king and can do no wrong. The customer of the computer industry was seen as the DP manager. The IT industry has recognized that its customer is not just the person who tends the computer mainframe. The key customer is the terminal user, and specifically the manager, who has a terminal in use on his own desk. This is important to the IT industry because the terminal market itself is worth many times the computer mainframe market. Realizing this, the IT industry will do everything it can to make its products, and computers in particular, easy to use. This is what the well-publicized Japanese 'fifth generation' development is all about.

Development will concentrate on the user's interaction with the computer. Some advances have already been made in this field and the manufacturers' sales literature is full of claims about the ease-of-use aspects of their products. There are already easy-to-use menu driven programs, which lead the user step by step through the facilities available to him. These are particularly important to the non-specialist manager.

Computers are already much easier to use than they were even ten years ago. There are major improvements still to come and they will fuel the IT revolution even further. A major limitation for most users at present is the need to use a keyboard to communicate with the computer. Lightpens are already in use to draw instructions direct on to a screen. The big breakthrough will come when you can speak directly to the computer in plain English – or Spanish, French, German, Russian, or whatever.

The capital per worker ratio

The Agrarian Revolution started a process which has put £50,000 worth of capital investment behind every agricultural worker in Britain and has reduced the agricultural workforce from over 95 per cent of the working population to about 2 per cent. The Industrial Revolution started a process which has put £40,000 of capital investment behind each production worker in Britain. At first this led to a dramatic move of the working population into factories. Now, as capital investment and productivity increase, the numbers in manufacturing industry, not just in Britain but throughout the developed world, are falling steeply.

The proportion of knowledge workers in the working population is high and increasing. A knowledge worker is someone who supplies knowledge, ideas, concepts and information to productive work rather than applying manual strength and dexterity. The application of knowledge is now a key factor of production in the advanced developed economies. There are great pressures to increase the productivity of knowledge workers.

The IT Revolution has started to impact on knowledge workers, ranging from clerks and typists to managers, technicians, and creative and professional people. The initial effect was the replacement of rooms full of clerks doing routine repetitive tasks by computers. More recently, word processing has speeded up the work of the typist and increased his or her productivity. Most of the capital investment for knowledge workers has been at the lower levels. The late eighties and nineties will see a major IT impact at the other end of the scale. Much greater power will be placed at the elbow of the manager and other professional knowledge workers. This power will give them access to more and better information and will enable them to manipulate it more effectively. One estimate suggests that by early in the twenty-first century each knowledge worker will be backed by the equivalent of £12 million worth of today's IT equipment. The actual investment will be only £1200 a head but each £1 will buy as much IT equipment as £1000 buys today. Can you imagine what you might do if you and every one of your staff were backed by £12 million worth of computing, telecommunications, and office equipment? Most of us cannot begin to think what the impact will be. We need to if we are to survive.

IT trends

We do not know for sure where the IT Revolution will take us or how it will develop. As productivity increases dramatically, will it be balanced by greater leisure or merely by enforced unemployment? Or are the needs and opportunities so great that, as in Victorian times, the new technology will be seized, put to work, and used to change every aspect of our society? Our concern here is with the key trends in IT and how they will alter the manager's job. The one thing that we can say with certainty is that every manager who hopes to continue in management needs to be aware of the IT Revolution and to keep abreast of developments and trends.

The introduction of computers has distorted the way in which we hold and handle information. Large expensive computers had to be fully used – round the clock for preference – so as to spread the capital investment overhead. This led to centralization of computing and information storage for reasons of control, economy, and organizational feasibility. This is unnatural. Most information is used at or near the point at which it enters an organization. Only summaries or selective items of information are needed elsewhere. Commonly, 40 per cent of information stored is needed by a specific individual or work group. Another 40 per cent is used within the same establishment or workplace. Only 20 per cent needs to leave the establishment. In large corporations and public sector organizations, very little of this is needed in the centre of the organization; perhaps less than 1 per cent. There is already a need for decentralization of information. As technological constraints are progressively removed, information will be stored close to the point of use – or at least made easily available there.

These pressures will be reinforced by user expectations. Users of all sorts in the field of knowledge work want better information to do their jobs more effectively and with greater satisfaction. They are no longer willing to be fobbed off with DP department excuses. They will not wait for years or even months for new systems. Nor are they prepared to accept delays of days, hours, or even minutes in obtaining the information they need to answer a customer query; carry forward a design stage; solve a production scheduling problem; decide whether a patient can safely be given a certain treatment; or decide whether a person found in suspicious circumstances should be arrested. Users want good information, that is information that is accurate, complete, up to date, and, above all, available at the time and place they need it. There is, and there will continue to be, pressure to provide information at the point of use. This may be from an individual desk-top computer or terminal linked through a network to databases containing the information needed for the user to do the job.

Most large organizations already have their own networks in place. These are systems linking computers and computer-held databases with terminals. They do this by electronic means and sometimes over considerable distances. Such networks need not be confined within the bounds of a single organization.

Videotex

Public videotex systems provide access from office or home to large databases of information. Among the simplest are the British television services, Ceefax and Oracle. They are provided through any TV set in the UK modified for the purpose. The user sits in front of his TV set with a keypad and, by pressing the appropriate keys, can call up a few thousand 'pages' of information on matters of general interest such as news, weather, road conditions, market prices, and sports news.

Larger-scale systems operate in several European countries – Prestel in the UK, Cept 3 in West Germany, and Antiope in France. The terminals for use with the systems are relatively inexpensive, based on the domestic TV set, and linked to extensive databases over the telephone network. The user pays a small charge for each page he looks at and pays the telephone charges for the call to the central computer. With Prestel the user has access to a more extensive store of information than with Ceefax or Oracle. He can, for instance, use the system to discover the cheapest available air fare to any destination. The terminals for videotex systems are becoming more elaborate. Already they are being used for two-way ('interactive') communication. On a limited scale, consumers can already select goods from a display on their TV screens, order them, and make payment from their bank or credit card account without ever getting out of their armchair. These systems are made possible by the collaboration of private undertakings in the retail and financial field with the public services network supplier.

Many firms have their own private videotex service, providing branch managers, for instance, with up-to-the-minute information about price and availability of goods. The Midlands region of the CEGB has such a service to provide up-to-date information about the state of the generating system for key managers and technicians. Such private systems can have links to each other or to public services like Prestel.

For some years British universities have shared their computer facilities through networks linking groups of universities together. These enable a terminal user to access a particular database whether it is on the computer at their campus or on another hundreds of miles away. The terminal user can also route his processing work to the particular computer on the network that has the power and facilities needed to do the work most effectively and economically.

Similarly some networks are used to provide specialist information to users, who subscribe to the service. The jargon for these services is Value Added Network Services or VANS. An example is the Telerate service which supplies terminals through which the financial community can obtain up-to-the-minute information from the world's financial markets. As technology improves and prices fall, more organizations will draw their customers into their networks with terminals that can be used to make enquiries, for example about delivery lead times and prices, and through which orders can be placed and even payment made. Already, as we have said, British Telecom, through its Prestel service, allows the private citizen to use his or her domestic TV set as a terminal for enquiry purposes and, to a limited extent, for placing orders with specific suppliers and for paying through the use of a credit card. Such services will clearly be greatly extended – for instance, to permit a direct debit to the customer's bank account. The local branches of large organizations in both the public and the private sector are increasingly being linked together by networks.

Local Area Networks

A more recent development is the Local Area Network or LAN. This is a coaxial or optical fibre cable laid as a simple ring throughout a building. A whole range of objects can be linked to the LAN, providing they meet the interface requirements. These objects can be computer nodes, peripherals, or terminals. They might, in due course, be electronic filing systems or copying machines. Each knowledge worker in the building can have his own terminal on his desk. This can have its own limited processing and storage facilities as well as providing normal telephone services.

Networks open up great possibilities for linking a wide range and variety of computing, telecommunications and office products. Providing Open Systems Interface standards are adhered to by manufacturers of IT equipment, this can be turned into a practical reality.

In the last thirty years many firms have found that they are tied to a single computer manufacturer. In practice they have been forced to stay with that manufacturer and to go on buying additional equipment from him or face the penalty of considerable disruption and cost as they make the transition to the equipment and standards of another supplier. These costs include retraining staff and changing attitudes and approaches.

Standards

The International Standards Organization published a networking framework standard in the early 1970s. This is known as the seven-layer model for open systems interconnection. Progress in adopting the standard was slow until the early 1980s when twenty leading European, Japanese and North American manufacturers of IT products – computers, telecommunications, and office systems equipment – adopted a common standard for Local Area Networks, known as the Open Systems LAN, covering the bottom four layers of the model. The adoption of this standard on a worldwide basis independent of technology is a significant milestone on the road to establishing true open systems interconnection and interworking between the equipment of different manufacturers. It will allow users to choose the best equipment for their purpose and to mix the best of each type on a single network.

The manager does not need to concern himself with the detail of the standards. However he should ensure that any IT equipment which he buys or which is supplied centrally for his department does conform to the open systems interconnection standards. The IT director or DP manager should welcome this attitude, though there may be some who have made such large investments in non-conforming equipment that they will resist. The benefits of open systems interconnection and interworking are immense. They protect the user's investment; allow him to add to and develop his network freely without having to abandon or drastically alter his existing systems. They provide him with a great measure of future flexibility, a fact of great importance in a rapidly changing business environment.

Databases

In the early days of computing, the emphasis in systems design was on the programs, which would do the work. The data was organized into specially structured files. Since then, the emphasis has moved to the organization of the data itself, as it was recognized that it was inefficient to input the same data several times and organize it into separate functional files, which can get out of step with each other. The database was evolved as a result of this perception. A company's data is organized and held in a database. The database can then be interrogated by a whole gamut of users, who select the data they need and then use their own program to manipulate it to produce the results they require. A database administrator maintains strict control over the database in order to prevent inadvertent or fraudulent tampering with the data.

At present, databases are generally centralized and controlled from one base. We can foresee that in the future each individual or work unit will hold its own database of information which it generates or uses frequently. The work unit will have access on a controlled basis to information which it needs less frequently and which is held elsewhere in the organization's distributed database. Similarly, key information needed by management and other units will be extracted from each work unit's database and held centrally. The difficulties of creating and controlling distributed databases effectively are considerable but we expect the technical problems to be overcome.

A number of important tools have been developed for use with databases. The Data Dictionary System (DDS) is the key tool, which provides considerable help in systems design as well as providing a map of the database. There are also standardized programs such as Querymaster and Reportmaster, which enable relatively unskilled users to integrate the database and produce simple formatted reports. A range of other productivity aids are being introduced by computer manufacturers to allow users to develop new application systems quickly and effectively. This can be particularly important when, for example, there are last minute changes in legislation affecting your firm.

Privacy legislation

One aspect of databases which will affect every manager is that of privacy legislation. Every country of the Western world has, or is introducing, legislation to protect individuals from inaccurate information being held about them in computer records. But this is a subject in itself and we devote a further chapter to it (see Chapter 19).

2 Understanding the market-place

Why marketing?

Why include marketing in a book about management? The answer is that every manager, whatever his function, needs to understand marketing and what it involves. We exist in a highly competitive environment where marketing is the key to survival. In this rapidly changing world, the marketing-led companies are the ones which survive and prosper. In a capitalist society or a mixed economy, companies are in business to make a profit. In the long run, a company will only make a profit if it satisfies the needs of the market. These are the companies that will survive. Very few entrepreneurs are totally insulated from competition.

Successful marketing lies at the heart of any commercial organization or indeed any organization supplying goods and services. A proper understanding of marketing is necessary to any manager who aspires to move upwards. In this chapter we seek to explain the nature of marketing in plain language and to show how every manager can contribute to the proper presentation of his firm and its products.

Many companies centre their thoughts on what they can develop or produce. They work on the theory that if they can produce better and cheaper goods or services, they must be successful. They become very production oriented. The managing director thumps home the lesson that if only the sales force can unload the steady stream of goods which his factories turn out all will be well. He can optimize the factory loading, reduce idle time for machinery and people, thus producing goods at minimum cost. Unfortunately, however, his calculations go astray if the sales force cannot push the goods on to a waiting public. They will only buy if they are convinced they need them. A pushing salesman may occasionally persuade someone to buy an item which he doesn't really want but he certainly won't succeed in making a steady stream of such sales. Broadly speaking, people only buy goods or services if they think they need them.

If research and development are concentrated on improving the product and on reducing cost, this is rewarding in the short term but may not be so in the long term. Many potential market needs are recognized and met by companies outside the field concerned. The need for better lighting and a more convenient and less messy means of supplying it may have been recognized by the makers of oil lamps. No doubt they worked hard at improving the wick, making a smoother feed for the wick, developing globes of a more effective shape and so on. However, totally new companies grew up to supply cheap and clean electric light and power. These innovations were based on developments made well outside the existing lighting lamp and oil supply companies.

The company which is marketing oriented tries to identify the needs, actual or potential, of the market. Having identified the needs, it tries to satisfy them. We speak of actual or potential needs because the customer may not clearly recognize his own needs. He may know that he wants better, cleaner lighting or warmer housing, or more reliable personal transportation, but have little clear idea of how the need may be met. The need may be even less well defined than that. The user may just recognize the irritating need to carry oil to his house to fill his lamps, or he may recognize the length of time it takes to starch and iron his collars. In the latter case, the need of the market was recognized by the growth of laundry service. However, the real market need was uncovered and exploited by the makers of nylon and similar artificial fibres. The drip dry shirt and other drip dry products not only satisfied the market needs but in the process caused severe problems for the laundry industry, which had set out to meet the need in a more obvious way.

It follows from this that the crucial step in the development of an idea into a new product or service lies not in the research laboratory but in identifying the market need. The successful company is imbued with the marketing approach. Market considerations impact upon every aspect of a company's activities. The same thing should also apply to nationalized industries and state corporations. We would also argue that it should apply to the work of local and central government departments. After all, most governments claim to operate 'for the people'. To illustrate the marketing concept at work we will consider how it works in practice.

Market research

Marketing we have said starts with the identification of customer needs. This is done by market research. Most companies do some form of market research even if they do not always recognize it as such. At the one extreme, the managing director's wife may give him her views on the company's products from time to time. At the other extreme, and particularly in large consumer products companies, there may be a large market research department making use of a wide range of techniques to try to establish the needs of the market.

It is in fact possible to carry out quite effective market research with only a very small department. If a company is an existing one, it is already directly in touch with a number of outlets for its goods. The sales force can feed back their views. If necessary the company can carry out a special survey to obtain their views. If the business is to provide goods or services for consumers, as opposed to supplying goods or services to industry and commerce, the staff and their families are consumers as well. Their views, where appropriate, can be obtained as part of the market research effort. In particular, they can be asked to act as guinea pigs to try out new or improved products.

Market research can involve a study of government statistics. For instance a manufacturer of prams is interested in statistics relating to births and size of family, and in government forecasts of future trends in this field. Similarly a number of commercial organizations may make forecasts and provide statistics which may be applied to market research for your company. Banks, serious newspapers and the trade press are possible starting points for facts and trends.

Elaborate questionnaires can be prepared and put to a typical cross-section of potential customers. We are all familiar with political polls and many people will remember how wildly inaccurate some poll predictions have been. Market research polls can be as easy way to spend a lot of money. The value of the research depends on a number of factors. First, the questions themselves must be very carefully thought out and must be completely unambiguous. Then, the cross-section must be

29

carefully selected. The results of a sample of, say, 1000 people questioned will purport to represent the views of possibly many millions of people. If the sample is not truly representative of the population being researched, then the final result will be likewise inaccurate. The smaller the sample that is taken, the more important it is to ensure that there is no bias in it. A random sample is not one carelessly selected at random. It is one which as nearly as possible represents the population of which it forms a part.

Test marketing is another tool of market research, again particularly in the consumer products field. A pilot production run is started with a new product, perhaps by selling the product in a limited geographical area. With simple capital equipment, early prototype models may be placed with existing customers. The object of the exercise in either case is to establish the market reaction to the new product. The result may be to modify the product, to put it into full production or even to withdraw it from the market.

Whatever method is adopted, one thing is certain: the real needs of the market must be established. A firm may go on for years, even for decades, making a product acknowledged to be the best of its kind. It may be convinced that market research is not necessary because its product is selling steadily and that is all the evidence that's needed. Perhaps another firm, possibly not even in the same line of business, may be alert to the needs of the market. That firm may come up with a product more nearly matched to the needs of the market than the product of the existing company. The result may well be a loss, temporary or permanent, of a significant part of the market. A case worth studying is that of the razor blade market – the rise of Wilkinson Sword and the stainless steel blade, and the subsequent development of the shaving products market.

Product planning

It is one thing to discover what the market need is. It is another to find a way to meet the need. New products and services may be developed directly as a result of market research having revealed a need which is not currently being met. The product planning department may set down a product aim, based on such research, and work forward until it can produce a plan for the production of a new product which meets the requirement. Many large companies approach their new product design in this way. Others merely follow a policy of 'continuous improvement' of existing products. One of the most difficult aspects of product planning is to take the results of research work or the development of new techniques and see how they can be used to satisfy the needs of the market. Yet identifying this link may be vital to the survival of a company or even of a country. The United Kingdom, for instance, spends an unusually high proportion of its gross national product on research, yet does not appear to reap the full advantage of this in the market-place. Much of the early research in the field of radar, computers, atomic power and jet engines was done in the UK. In many of these fields some of the most advanced research in the world is still being done in the UK. Yet the UK by no means dominates the market in these fields. The reason lies in the marketing gap. Many UK companies in these fields are slow to see the real needs of their customers. They are more concerned with seeking perfection than in making use of the current state of development to meet those customer needs.

The company which launches a good product, which meets the users' needs, may well saturate the market and prevent the company with a far better product ever getting a decent share of the market, because the better product is too slow getting off the mark. It is also true that companies have slogged on developing and introducing an advanced product only to see a marketing conscious company come into the industry at a later stage in the game, adapt the ideas of the early birds more closely to the needs of the market and sweep the board. Whatever form a product planning department takes and wherever it fits into the company hierarchy, it has to remember that it only stays in business if its new products satisfy the needs of the market.

Advertising and promotion

One aspect of marketing which everyone knows about is advertising and promotion. Promotion embraces all those plastic toys in the breakfast cereals and the super competitions which you can enter free, so long as your entry is accompanied by labels or carton tops from the product being promoted.

There are those who think that advertising will sell anything. This is just not so. Advertising will only sell if it is selling a product which meets a market need. The need does not have to be a tangible one. Much of the advertising we see today trades on our need for acceptance and for security.

Advertising must be informative, it must carry a positive message, even if the message is little more than a brand name and an associated picture of effectiveness. It does not pay to try to be too clever. People may never get beyond the negative part of the message in captions like 'Don't buy our booze because . . .' They may miss the clever ending, which has the advertising agency in stitches. Similarly it is a golden rule never to mention your competitors in your advertisements. Why give them free publicity? Even knocking copy helps to draw their name to the attention of the public.

Choice of advertising media can be of critical importance. Common sense may tell you whether to advertise a pornographic novel in the *Church Times* or a highbrow novel in the *Daily Mirror*. Day-to-day decisions on where to advertise can be more tricky. You are simply trying to reach the maximum number of people who might seriously consider buying your product, at the minimum cost per head. Evaluating the alternatives can be quite complicated and some advertising agencies use computers to help them.

Everybody naturally considers themselves to be experts in advertising. In some companies a senior manager vets the proposed advertising. He may consult some of his colleagues, his secretary and maybe even his wife. The final advertisement becomes an unfortunate compromise between the original professionally produced job and the amateur improvements on it. The proverb applies in this field as in many others: Don't own a dog and bark yourself.

Price

Price is one of the most important factors in marketing. The simple approach to pricing is to work out the costs and add a margin to cover overheads, risk and profit. If the sales manager says the price is too high for him to sell the product and that it must be reduced by 20 per cent, then the production manager points out that if he increases production by 50 per cent he can reduce costs and hence price by the required 20 per cent.

This is illustrative of the wrong way to fix prices. First, if your company makes several different products, it is very difficult to establish the true costs. It is also difficult to establish what overheads are rightly attributable to this product. If the sales manager was right in thinking he could sell the original number at the lower price, he may well be unable to sell the higher number to which he has committed himself in order to obtain the low price.

The volume of sales normally bears some relationship to price. The demand for some items doesn't vary much according to price. An example is salt. You would probably use as much as you do now if the price were halved, doubled or even multiplied by ten. Economists describe such items as being subject to inelastic demand. Other items are very price sensitive, for instance the volume of sales of lemons varies with price. Economists assume that the buyer will, other things being equal, always buy his goods at the lowest possible price. This is in practice not always so, because goods are generally different in some way or other, if only in the packaging. In addition, buyers, for one reason or another, do not always buy the cheapest goods. The man who buys a Rolls Royce car and the woman who buys a dress from a fashion house are not looking for cheapness. Even in the industrial field a buyer may rate reliability, good service or a good reputation more highly than cheapness. He may also be more concerned with the total cost of ownership, including operation and maintenance over the item's life, than with the immediate cost of purchase.

Ideally the price should be decided according to a marketing view of what is possible. Whereas the typical salesman likes to be able to offer the lowest price, the marketing man tries to produce a product which most closely fits the needs of the market. Also, in setting the price, he is more concerned with total profit from sales rather than with the highest volume of sales.

Commercial policy

Closely linked with the question of price is that of commercial policy. Is the company going to deal directly with the end user or is there to be an intermediary? With consumer goods there may be wholesalers and retailers. For capital goods there may be agency arrangements. Where there are intermediaries a decision must be made on their reward. It must be adequate and there may be a case for making it sufficiently attractive for them to want to push your product at the expense of your competitors'.

What will the price cover? Will it include any element for instruction manuals or for after-sales service? Is it better to have a higher price and spend more on advertising? Should there be any difference in the marketing of the product in different segments of the market? Should any customers be given preferential treatment? For instance, customers buying a high volume may be offered a discount. A tyre manufacturer may offer a preferential price to a motor car manufacturer not only because of the size of the order but also because of the advertising value of having his tyres fitted as original equipment. There is also the hope that when the tyres need replacing the owner of the car may be idle and buy straight replacements rather than shop around.

Distribution and selling

Distribution and sales are the final stage of marketing and not, as some people believe, the whole of marketing. This is not to disparage sales. There is more to it than sending out fast talkers with a strong foot for putting in doors. Methods of distribution have to be decided on. If distribution is to be from depots, then those depots have to be sited to best advantage. Large modern companies use mathematical and computer techniques to help them make the decision. Sales managers are constantly exercised by the problem of how to cover the prospects effectively. How can prospective customers be identified? How should sales territories be defined? Should they be on a geographical basis or divided in some other way, for example by particular classes of customer?

In sales, as in other areas, the 80/20 per cent rule applies. It is quite common for 80 per cent of the value of orders to come from 20 per cent of customers. It is also quite common for 80 per cent of sales to be made by 20 per cent of the salesmen. These are, of course, generalizations, but they contain more than an element of truth. Effective sales management examines this situation. It may be that some marginal customers are not worth retaining. They may cost more to sell to than they bring in. Similarly the profit on the business which some salesmen bring in may not justify their salary and expenses.

Public relations

Every company is or should be concerned about its public image.

The same should be true of nationalized industries, government departments and local authorities. A company which is well thought of finds it easier than others to retain the loyalty of its customers, to recruit staff and obtain co-operation from central government and local authorities. Above all, a good reputation, resulting from good public relations, helps to produce repeat orders and new customers.

Good public relations are not just a matter for the public relations officer or some public relations firm. It is an area in which every manager and every employee can play an important part. People judge a company not first by its product or its advertising, but by the behaviour of its staff, and especially by the behaviour of its managers. Whenever a manager formally meets someone outside the company, he is being judged as the representative of the company. This is true whether he is meeting a customer, a prospective customer, an applicant for a job, a supplier, or a visitor from the local technical college or local authority. People also judge on casual meetings. If you see a stranger in the reception area, when no receptionist is about, ask if you can help. Do the same if you find a stranger looking lost in the office corridor.

It is surprising how far opinion is influenced by casual comments in unguarded moments. Be careful in the local pub or restaurant at lunch time not to disparage your company so that people can hear. The chief engineer may be a bumbling incompetent old idiot but you should avoid the temptation to say so in public.

Your contribution

Your attitude should be more positive than just guarding against indiscretions. You should set out, without flamboyant over-emphasis, to speak well of your company and its products, whenever the opportunity presents itself.

If you can see a market need which you believe your company could fulfil, do something about it, if it is only to put a note down about it to your market research department or to your own manager. You may be told that your idea has been thought of many times before, but don't be discouraged. The man who doesn't make a move doesn't put a foot wrong. The manager who is going to make a contribution to his company takes a broad view

35

and tries to see beyond the narrow confines of his own immediate job. Meeting the needs of the market is essential for every successful company. It is vital for every manager in the company.

Marketing

We have written briefly about the various aspects of marketing because we feel that marketing lies at the heart of any successful company. Every manager should know something about marketing. In particular he should think about the needs of his company's customers and how they can be satisfied.

3 Organizations and change

Managers need to understand organizations. Organizations are all pervasive; we meet them in all aspects of our life – football clubs, schools, churches, residents' associations, rotary clubs, local choirs and orchestras, political parties and parent teacher associations. We also meet them every day at work in our own firms and in the firms and public sector organizations with which we deal. Our concern here is with those organizations established for economic reasons – businesses operating for profit – and organizations which provide a public service.

Rudyard Kipling wrote 'He travels the fastest, who travels alone'. Yet there are a great many things that an individual cannot achieve on his own. This may be from lack of adequate physical strength, lack of the necessary range of skills, or lack of money to provide the necessary equipment and to fund the day-to-day operations. Organizations provide the framework within which individuals can co-operate together to achieve what they could not achieve on their own.

Organizations should bring about synergy. In primary school we learn that $1 + 1 = 2$. Where synergy exists, this is no longer true. The whole is greater than the sum of the parts, so $1 + 1 = 3$. It is the aim of the successful organization always to achieve the highest degree of synergy possible – both synergy between individuals and synergy between the parts of the organization.

Organizational objectives

Every organization has a reason for its existence. Its prime objective may be profit or public service, but it will, in practice, have a whole hierarchy of objectives. The prime objective of profit will be quantified and split down in at least two different ways. It will be split by activity and by time. Thus the profit objective of the retail activity may be different from the profit objective of the wholesale activity. There may be different profit objectives for this week, this year, next year, and each year for five or more years ahead. The short-term objectives will be clear and well defined. Longer-term objectives may well be conceptual or even visionary in nature.

In considering the nature of an organization's hierarchy of objectives there is one vital principle that must always be observed if the organization is to be successful. The organization's objectives must reinforce the individual objectives of the people who make up the organization, and their individual objectives must reinforce the organization's objectives. In other words, organizational and individual objectives must be compatible. This will be achieved partly by the conditions of service established for individual members of an organization, but it is also an important consideration in the design of organizations.

Traditional organizations

The traditional forms of organization are authoritarian and hierarchical. Military organization is typical of the traditional style: one man commands a unit and there is a direct chain of command down through a pyramid of sub-unit commanders to the private soldiers at the base of the pyramid. There is no ambiguity about it. Every man in the organization has one boss and one boss only and orders flow quickly and smoothly down through the chain of command. Figure 1 illustrates this.

Most business organizations are based on the principles of the traditional or hierarchical organization. These are:

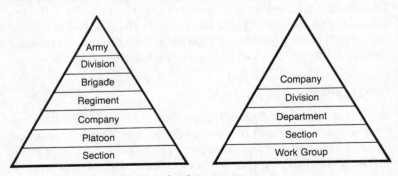

Figure 1 A traditional organization

- Each man or woman looks to only one person in the organization for his or her instructions.
- The number of people whom any one manager can control is limited. For a mixed team with each subordinate handling a different type of work, the limit is probably five or six. Where the subordinates are doing identical work, the span of control can go up to thirty or more.
- Chains of command are kept as short as possible. Long chains of command lead to distortion of information flows.

Such an organization is ideal for fairly rigid control of a firm. It is, however, fairly inflexible and cannot react swiftly to change.

The traditional division of labour in industry is:

Development
Manufacturing
Marketing
Accounts and administration

As companies become larger each of these departments is divided into smaller and smaller specialties. The Marketing Department may spawn a Sales Department. As the firm grows this may be divided into Home and Overseas Sales Departments. In a very large company the Home Sales Department may be divided into several sales regions, each divided into several sales branches, which in turn are divided into sales areas.

Organization charts

Company organizations are usually represented in the form of organization charts. A simple chart is shown in Figure 2. One of the disadvantages of this sort of chart is that one man appears to be above another to be a superior person. No one likes to think of themselves as being 'below' another. One managing director tried to get around this by drawing his organization chart in the form shown in Figure 3. Instructions and direction flowed from left to right. No significance was attached to vertical position which, as far as possible, was arranged from top to bottom in alphabetical order.

It is necessary to publish organization charts in companies of any size. If a chart is not published there is a danger of confusion. This may be slight in a company employing only a few people. By

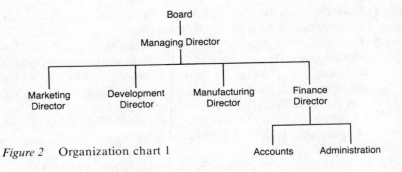

Figure 2   Organization chart 1

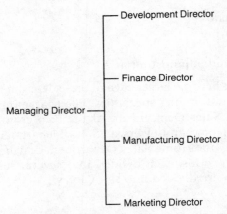

Figure 3   Organization chart 2

the time it employs a hundred, the organization chart is likely to be essential. Even if each manager knows what he himself is responsible for, there is a danger of overlap and also of gaps between the boundaries of individual authority. A good organization chart helps to highlight such gaps and overlaps. This should lead to action to rectify the organizational weakness. Regrettably, the mere publication of an organization chart can lead to a degree of ossification within an organization. The organization becomes enshrined in the chart and no responsibility can change until it has been duly accepted as an amendment to the chart. Any reasonably flexible company publishes its charts in looseleaf form.

In practice few modern companies can be as simple as the one illustrated in Figures 2 and 3. These show a simple line relationship. The superior's authority is direct and his authority is general. However, other forms of relationship are necessary in an organization. Staff relationships provide for advice from specialists. Thus a design consultant may hold a staff appointment and provide advice across all departments of a company. Functional relationships provide for a specialist to have authority within the organization for certain specific activities. For instance, every advertisement placed by any person in the organization may have to be approved by the Public Relations and Advertising Manager even if it is a recruitment advertisement in a local newspaper. Similarly the Data Processing Manager might have authority to approve or disapprove the purchase of any computing equipment in the organization. Thus a departmental manager who wished to buy a micro to sit on his desk would have to obtain the DP Manager's approval before he made the purchase, even though the cost might be within his normal budget authority.

Changing organizational style

Fixed organizations tend to put blinkers on people. Middle and junior managers may lose sight of the real aims of the company as they concentrate on their own area of responsibility. To overcome the problems of rigidity and reduction in individual responsibility, two trends are discernible.

First there is an attempt to break down large organizations into smaller self-accounting, self-driving units which are complete in themselves. The units specialize in one area of the company's business. They have all the functions – development, production, marketing, field service, and administration – which they need to operate. They have their own general manager or managing director, who runs them with minimum guidance from the parent company. Such units may even have their own subsidiary board. Such a board probably is made up of executives from the parent company with maybe one or two non-executive directors from outside the company to give a broader understanding of the business world. On a less grand scale, a large degree of autonomy may be given to branch managers within a retail chain.

The other noticeable trend is the attempt to move away from authoritarian organizations to very flexible ones where roles change as the requirements of the situation demand. This may involve the extensive use of project teams or task forces set up to handle a specific task. On completion of the task, the team or task force is disbanded and the staff move into another team or task force set up to handle a new task.

The one thing we can be sure about is that the perfect organization has not yet been evolved and probably never will be. Organizations evolve to meet the particular needs of an individual company or public service outfit. There is no universal solution. The demands on a commercial bank with hundreds of branches differ from those on a specialized merchant bank. Both differ from the demands on an engineering-based manufacturing company or a software house.

Company organization has to adapt to meet changes in the external environment. The impact of external influences – shareholders, customers, suppliers, trade unions, recruitment sources, local and central government – will be reflected in the company organization.

Designing a new organization

Managers sometimes have to design a new organization. This may be for many reasons. Your firm may decide to enter a new market or to merge two existing activities. It may decide that a collection of separate activities should be brought together under one manager. Some activity may become so important that it warrants the creation of a new department. A manager may even look at his existing department and decide that it would perform better if it were reorganized.

When you set up a new organization, start by asking yourself some questions. What is the purpose of the new organization? What are its objectives? What is the environment within which it will exist? What activities are necessary to achieve the objectives? What external and internal links will have to be serviced? Will it operate as a profit centre or as a cost centre? The answers to these questions may be contained in your brief or you may have to work them out for yourself. If you work in a large organization, you will need to agree the answers with your own manager. If you are setting up your own independent organization, you will need to ask yourself a number of more fundamental questions about the viability and prospective profitability of your proposed new organization. These will include questions about the market and about the availability of capital.

When you have answered these questions satisfactorily you will need to assess the likely scale of activity. This may be done, for instance, by looking at the target objectives for turnover or profit. In the public service you might scale from an appropriate measure such as the number of transactions to be handled. From the scale and type of operation you will know whether your new organization is likely to require twenty or two hundred people. The number of people will impact on the design of the organization.

At this stage, you look at the activities that the organization will have to perform and the objectives. Group the activities together in a logical way. Then try to split your objectives down into a hierarchy which can be matched with the groups of activities. Make each sub-unit responsible for a complete range of activity contributing to the whole, rather than for a mere specialist slice of activity. The more complete the activity which you give to the sub-unit, the clearer the objectives of that sub-unit can be, and the stronger the chance that you will be able to obtain real commitment from the people of the sub-unit.

In practice, you may have severe constraints put on your freedom to design a new unit's organization. You may have to accept functioning sections from other parts of the company into it. You may have to accept a unit from a company which your firm has taken over. You may have to accept into the new unit existing staff with limited skills. All these will constrain your design.

In designing a new organization, whatever the constraints, seek to achieve the following:

- An organization where the individual's objectives can be in harmony with the organization's objectives and *vice versa*.
- An organization which can be controlled.
- The delegation of as much authority as possible.
- The shortest possible lines of communication and hence as few layers of management as practicable.
- The smallest possible allocation of resources to overhead activities.

Organizational dangers

Organizations, like individuals, may be good, bad, or indifferent.

They may be well suited to their purpose when they are first established, but may become inflexible and set in their ways. Most organizations face three main dangers:

1 They may develop fat.
2 Communication may become slow and difficult.
3 They may lose sight of their purpose and decision making may become very difficult.

One could argue that these are merely three symptoms of the same disease.

The people in an organization can be divided broadly into those who do the real work – developing, designing, marketing, distributing, selling, and servicing – and those who constitute overheads – administration, planning, personnel and one hundred and one other specialist functions. Overhead functions are essential but they have a habit of expanding and proliferating. It is difficult to measure their contribution. Many measures which are devised to assess their contribution are highly artificial and easy to fudge.

Many overhead functions are highly specialized. A firm may need expertise in foreign exchange, customs and excise procedures, data protection and privacy, pension fund administration, export credits, or industrial relations law. Many of these functions can be contracted out to specialist firms, or a manager may develop enough knowledge to cover the subject part-time. In many cases, particularly in a medium-sized firm, a specialist may be employed because it is felt that the subject is too important to the firm for it to be handled on an amateur basis or by people from outside the firm. The firm may thus employ a specialist even though there is not enough work to keep him fully employed. The real job may take up only half or even a third of his time. The rest of his time is available for other use. Many such people devote this time relatively harmlessly to attending external seminars, writing papers for specialist journals, generally becoming involved in the affairs of their profession, or even playing golf. Others, more dangerously, write memos, call meetings and attend other people's meetings unnecessarily. In doing so they not only use up their own time, but they also make significant calls on the time of other people within the organization. The worst aspect of this is when the under-employed specialist starts calling for returns from the working units or setting up meetings at which they are required to be represented. The specialist is then actively reducing the productivity of the working units.

The problem can be just as great when a specialist finds that he has more work to do than he can manage in the time available. He might pass his less specialist work on to another department. He might propose that his job is split into two and one half given to another specialist. He is more likely to propose that he is given an assistant. He will have to spend time in managing the assistant and it will not be long before he needs a second assistant and starts to build up a regular department. The staff are less skilled than he is and so he devotes more and more of his time to managing, and less and less to exercising his specialist skills. The overhead load grows and the service deteriorates.

Empire building is not confined to the overhead departments. Many managers judge their status by the number of people they manage. Fortunately the effects of empire building in working units are seen more immediately in the business ratios for the unit.

The fatter an organization becomes, the more effort is needed for co-ordination and other non-productive tasks. Communication becomes more difficult as more layers of management have to be penetrated and more specialist departments consulted before any action can be taken.

Interdepartmental rivalries flourish and it can become more important to score a point over a rival department, or to protect one's territory, than to achieve the company's objectives. 'Idle hands make mischief' says the old proverb. To avoid idle hands, it is vital to prevent the growth of fat in an organization. Further, it is necessary to seek constantly for greater productivity from existing staff. As an aid to this, it is desirable to audit an organization from time to time and make each manager justify his department and every post within it.

Our own part

Most of us work in fairly rigid organizations, but we recognize that life is not rigid and inflexible. We adjust and adapt to the organization within which we work. In the process we modify the working of the organization. An informal organization grows up within the formal one. The informal organization reflects reality: it takes account of which sleepy managers should be bypassed; it recognizes that some managers and some departments abdicate from their responsibilities. The boundaries laid out so rigorously in theory can be crossed in practice.

One barrier to communication across organizational boundaries is suspicion and mistrust. Try to overcome this so far as your own department is concerned. One way of doing so is to attach your people, for periods of a few days or weeks, to the departments they have to deal with. It makes it a lot easier for them to get things done if they have met, worked, eaten and drunk with the people concerned. It also pays to welcome people from other parts of the company on day visits or attachments to your department. Where your work is very dependent on the work of another department, regular two-way visits and attachments should be fostered. If your company has an active sports life, encourage your people to develop their contacts in the club.

You should spend an appreciable amount of time developing your own contacts across the company's organizational boundaries. Go out of your way to visit other parts of the company. Welcome visitors yourself and make a point of making them feel welcome. If they come unannounced, find time to talk to them and give them a cup of coffee. If they come at the appropriate time, go out to lunch with them. If other departments ask for your help, give it even if it causes you considerable inconvenience. Invitations from the sales force to talk to customers or prospective customers should be accepted wherever possible. Be prepared at any time to talk about your work and that of your department. It will probably be worth-while to have a set of lecture notes and visual aids so that you can give such talks at short notice.

Recognize that conflict exists in organizations. There may well be a conflict of interest between managers. In large companies many managers' interests may legitimately conflict. Superimposed on this is the conflict arising from personal ambitions and jealousies. No manager should be surprised at the existence of these conflicts. If you are prepared for them you can help to resolve them. The informal links that you have established will help you to do this. Organizations exist to help us achieve our objectives, not to get in the way.

PART 2

Managing yourself

4 Be effective — be successful

What must a manager achieve?

To be successful we must be effective. We must have the drive to succeed and we must learn the basic rules of effectiveness. Look around at successful people you know or that you read about in business, sport or entertainment. You will find that in all cases, although some may have in-built gifts, all got to where they are by learning to be effective at the thing they do. 'Practice makes perfect' is an old adage. It is just as applicable to the effective manager as to any other person. We take it for granted that a footballer, boxer, runner or pianist has to practice over and over again to become the effective practitioner of his sport or profession. Strangely enough, many people have the total misconception that to be a manager all you need is just a room, a carpet on the floor and a name on the door. It is possible, of course, for some form of management to be carried out by virtually anybody, but here we are concerned with effective management. We can illustrate the difference between effective and non-effective managers. What we cannot give you is your determination to succeed.

The measure of effectiveness

First we need a simple description of effectiveness which is clear and unambiguous. It is:

The measure of effectiveness is how well a manager achieves the agreed objectives for his position

This is his real task. Note that it is not what he is, or what he does, but what he achieves, for example:

What I am	Manager of a small sales force
What I do	Sell products X and Y
What I must achieve	Expand sales of products X and Y by 10 per cent this year without increasing my selling costs.

An insurance friend of ours, when talking about this question of achievement, said 'I could simply say I am an area manager and I look after six salesmen, but I know my real job is to plan ahead, and encourage and guide my men so that we all meet our targets. I'm lucky, we not only have the targets but also the incentive that every £1000 sold means a useful addition to my income and pension. Not everyone has this added incentive.'

A manufacturing manager had achievement in mind when he said 'It's not only so many units produced per year, but ensuring we meet targets of time-scale, cost, quality and reliability as well. Then we can say we are really achieving our objectives and making a contribution to the company.

Some of you may say that in your particular job it is too difficult to set objectives and hence measure achievements. With some jobs it is difficult, especially if the end result cannot be measured quantitatively. Whatever your job, think: what can I do that really benefits my company, however small it may be, something that will add to its overall achievements? Remember, only the 'what I must achieve' is meaningful in terms of effective management.

Efficiency versus effectiveness

Efficiency is not the same as effectiveness. A divisional manager we know in a large wholesaling company has the most untidy desk you can imagine. His secretary long ago gave up trying to keep it tidy, yet this man is effective; he is an expert at his job; he looks ahead; he plans; he initiates new profitable products and ruthlessly cuts out any problem ones; he meets his targets of expansion and profits. In short, he is an effective manager. Some people in the company find him difficult because he is not sympathetic to pettiness and time-wasting. They find his office an eyesore. His company's board of directors find him a tower of strength.

Now before you accuse us of believing in sloppy offices which we don't, we tell this little tale to point the moral that being tidy is not being effective. We do not confuse tidy conformity with effectiveness. In one company we visited we were shown with great pride the invoicing department. The area shone with neatness and cleanliness and we thought what a pleasant place it was. We talked with the manager about his staff and his productivity. The manager spoke at length about the invoicing work and how busy they were, how he would have to get extra help again soon and so on. Not once did he discuss the productivity question.

Another manager might have said 'The job here is to prepare invoices and to see that the lowest cost per invoice is achieved, while maintaining the quality and accuracy of the work.'

In this example it is clear that higher management were not being effective in allowing the manager to be so ignorant of his duty to improve productivity.

The basic rules

Once you have decided that you are going to succeed in management, then the next job is to learn the basic rules. First and foremost must come management of yourself. You have to manage yourself effectively because no amount of ability, skill, experience or knowledge will in itself make you an effective executive. Effective management is far more than managing the work of others. Like many professions, it consists of a system of disciplines which, when learned thoroughly and practised assiduously, will fit most people for a higher level than that at which they now find themselves.

Effective management therefore can be learned, given a basis of knowledge and intelligence.

Remove the deadwood

You know the sort of deadwood that gathers in a management job: unnecessary correspondence, unnecessary meetings, jobs which your staff can do as well as you (perhaps better!), minor decisions which someone else could take, and a thousand and one other time-wasters. Learn how to distinguish the wood from the trees and you are most likely to be able to see, for example, the advantages of technological change and exploit the opportunities that could arise. In the deadwood also comes the work that will no longer be productive: the project which is not going to achieve

51

anything for the company, no experience, no profit or which is making too low a profit. Our expectations of projects change with time. The most cherished ones sometimes have to be killed in order to release resources for a more profitable project. We have to recognize the good from the bad and clear any deadwood away. One managing director told us 'One of the big weaknesses in many managers is carrying on with jobs that will clearly not help the company results. Like the shopkeeper we must clear out the non-productive lines.'

Spend your time effectively

We shall tell you much more about time and how to use it, but the important thing to realize is that the maximum time must be used for the really important jobs. It is only too easy to fritter time away on unimportant matters. We all know the grasshopper man who jumps from job to job crying 'I'm so busy I haven't time to do my job properly'. The lack of time is because he is not busy doing the right work in the right time.

Do what you do well

If you use your time correctly, you will pick out the key jobs and you must then do them well. Success does not come from running every race, it comes from winning the races you enter. In learning how to do what we do well we ought to widen our general business knowledge so that our business acumen and entrepreneurial flair has a chance to grow.

Make effective decisions

Decisions have to be meaningful. You have heard the man who boasts that he always makes a decision, and quickly. Decisions are of course necessary. They are important and a manager has to be prepared to make them, but they do not need to be made rashly. Remember that the right decision is often to consider whether the question was right, not just to answer it. We need to learn to make short-term tactical decisions without detriment to longer-term strategic issues.

Think about change

Keep some of your time for thinking about new ideas and testing them out in your job. We must develop the ability to introduce new methods. It requires the ability to persuade other people to adopt your ideas, not least your company.

Plan to be effective

Like any other task, the system of effective management requires a plan to make it happen. The planning is largely 'management by objectives'. This simply means that the objectives of any managerial task are stated in advance. They are agreed objectives in that the manager concerned agrees them in advance with his own senior manager. The tasks must have a high probability of successful completion by proper planning, and they must be difficult enough to draw out the best in all the staff concerned. We then finish up with the company having a complete corporate plan, and agreed objectives with all managers. This does not mean that managers are then in a straitjacket, but that targets exist in the company for all to strive for. This gives the best chance of success and fosters the growth of management skills.

The total plan is formulated by the company in the light of past achievements and its hopes for the future. The subject of corporate planning is outside the scope of this book, but what can be said is that a plan must exist to include the targets for turnover, profit, expenditure, manpower, product development and, above all, cash flow, for up to five years ahead (in many businesses). In some, the planning may extend to ten or fifteen years. The planning will be on a continuous basis, updated each year. More or less irrevocable commitment to expenditure on plant and materials may have to take place before delivery, in some cases several years. Monitoring of the shorter-term planning will take place at regular intervals and any adjustments will be made to the plan accordingly.

Different businesses have different problems, for example: a chain store is planning far ahead to find suitable sites for new stores; a software house is planning to market a new range of software and there will be planning problems, particularly with staff and marketing; a wholesale company will be looking at least eighteen months ahead, possibly abroad, for new ranges of goods it can sell; or a finance house may be looking at the effects of possible future money rate changes on its cash flow.

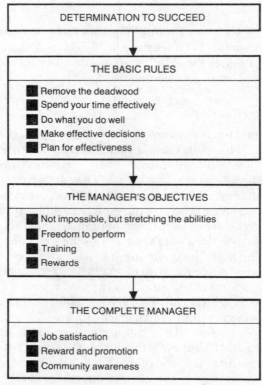

```
┌─────────────────────────────────────────┐
│        DETERMINATION TO SUCCEED           │
└─────────────────────────────────────────┘
                    │
                    ▼
┌─────────────────────────────────────────┐
│             THE BASIC RULES               │
├─────────────────────────────────────────┤
│  ■ Remove the deadwood                    │
│  ■ Spend your time effectively            │
│  ■ Do what you do well                    │
│  ■ Make effective decisions               │
│  ■ Plan for effectiveness                 │
└─────────────────────────────────────────┘
                    │
                    ▼
┌─────────────────────────────────────────┐
│         THE MANAGER'S OBJECTIVES          │
├─────────────────────────────────────────┤
│  ■ Not impossible, but stretching the     │
│    abilities                              │
│  ■ Freedom to perform                     │
│  ■ Training                               │
│  ■ Rewards                                │
└─────────────────────────────────────────┘
                    │
                    ▼
┌─────────────────────────────────────────┐
│           THE COMPLETE MANAGER            │
├─────────────────────────────────────────┤
│  ■ Job satisfaction                       │
│  ■ Reward and promotion                   │
│  ■ Community awareness                    │
└─────────────────────────────────────────┘
```

Figure 4   The effective manager

All companies are, or should be, planning their way ahead. As a manager, each one of us has some part to play in setting the overall targets for our company and setting out to achieve or better them.

The manager's objectives

We have seen how all the objectives fit together to form the company plan. What about our little bit of this? We must try to achieve the following (see also Figure 4):

- The agreed objectives must be hard enough but not impossible. If they look impossible, try to explain logically why this is so. Don't try for easy targets, however: your own development as a manager will suffer.

54

- You must have freedom to perform. You must endeavour to be allowed to do the job in your own way. You know what you have to achieve. The resources you need will have been broadly agreed beforehand.
- Find out about any company training. If it looks sensible to improve your skills by attending a training course, try and do so. Don't, however, turn into a course absentee. You will be found out eventually.
- The reward and promotion you hope for if you do your job well is not entirely under your control. We hope your company is such that rewards are given to those who deserve them and not shared with non-performers, otherwise incentive is lost and merit goes unrewarded.

5 Managing your time: use it — not abuse it

1440 minutes - no more - no less

A great part of our time is spent at work and, for most of us, earning money. To appreciate what we do with our time we need to take a close look at a bit of it. Let us choose a day, since it is a complete unit. We work, eat and sleep, all in one day.

Is there any difference between your day and anyone else's day? The first reaction, perhaps, is to think about what each does in the day, and the answer would be yes, there must be a difference. One thing, however, is the same, and we can start from this fundamental premise. Each of us has in each day 1440 minutes, no more and no less. At the end of the day they are gone, never to return. But, we may argue, there is another day. There is another, but not this one that has just gone. This is the first and most important realization that we must all come to accept. There will not be another day to make up for today, whether it has been good, bad or indifferent.

This does not mean we all have to rush into nervous hysteria to try to account for every one of these precious minutes. Not at all. What it does mean is that we must become more conscious of time. Once we have achieved this real consciousness of time and what we do with it, or, more important, what we *can* do with it, we are able to take the next step in the management of our own time.

Work

Work consists of a mixture of jobs. some must be done today, some can, or must, wait; some are not really jobs at all; some are expected, some unexpected; some pleasant and some boring or unpleasant. Some jobs will take more than a day, some less. There are subdivisions *ad nauseam*.

How do we set about deciding what to do in a day? As managers

56

we are expected, in varying degrees, to make this choice for ourselves. There can be a bewildering lot of possibilities, all apparently required at once. Do we see Mr Evans who wants to talk to us urgently about a personal problem? Do we get out with a salesman who wants help with a new contact? Do we write the report that our manager is requesting as urgent? Do we get down to concentrate on a technical problem? When can we clear that mounting mail in the in-tray? What do we do?

Firstly we have to train ourselves so that we are not conscious of a mass of jobs waiting to be done. This is not easy to begin with, but there is a method to get on top of work. Use time properly, all 1440 minutes of it each day. Less sleep, of course, which most authorities on the subject tell us demands 8 hours or 480 minutes. That leaves 960 minutes. (We will come to the eating part later!)

Allocation of time

It depends, of course, what level of management we are at as to how we may ultimately allocate our time, but at all levels of management certain basic rules apply. The allocation of time does not imply that all jobs have to be included. In fact, the first rule is:

Always take the top few jobs which will have the greatest impact and get them done first. Don't waste precious minutes on minor jobs that somebody else can do or that produce less benefit for the company and its people. It is generally accepted that the 80/20 rule holds good in many parts of the business world:

20 per cent of sales represent 80 per cent of the sales volume
20 per cent of parts purchased cost 80 per cent of the total

In exactly the same way you will find that only 20 per cent or less of your tasks are the really important ones and should demand the greater part of your time. The rest can be done in the time that is left. The accent must be on your contribution to the good of the company and its staff.

Job order

What main tasks must come first? As far as possible the main grouping must be:

57

- Your staff
- Your customers
- The rest

These are the broad principles. Sometimes there will be difficulty in adhering to them; it is not a perfect world. Your staff must come first because you need them to make sure your department, and from this your company, is doing the job it was formed to do. This may be sales, research, production or project management, etc. To perform any of these functions demands that your staff are properly used, paid, housed and trained. It does not mean mollycoddling, but it does mean an intelligent, adult and businesslike relationship. After the broad principles, what about your own more detailed order of doing work? This will become clear when work planning has been dealt with, but there is one general rule in choosing the job order. There will often be tough jobs that demand a great deal of thought and tiring mental effort. Choose the time for these tasks when you are most alert, probably first thing in the morning.

Work planning

Selecting jobs must not be random. You need a plan of work. Set yourself targets. Today I will do this! If you do this planning every day for a period ahead, you will acquire capacity for doing more and more work. Here is the next rule then:

Plan your work. Make tight but achievable targets for yourself. Don't let jobs run on. Break up your day into intervals of time that you can fit and measure against individual jobs. Don't allocate time out of proportion to the importance of the job.

When you have done this for a week or two, you will appreciate that you are doing much more real work than you used to.

It is interesting to watch ourselves and others planning instinctively the steps in, say, catching a long-distance train or plane. Most people, though not all, we admit, will immediately formulate a plan. Arrive a little before needed, allow time to get to the station, fix the time to leave home or office. Invariably, we keep to these timetables. Bring the same disciplines to bear in work planning. In your planning you must leave some time for contingencies and also arrange for standby or fill-in jobs so that

58

if you do better than planned you can fill in with something else. Likewise, if contingencies *don't* arise.

Here is a very common contingency: if you have callers who are not on today's schedule, weigh the importance of their call against today's time. Never be rude, always polite. Listen and talk interestedly and be helpful, but do not settle in your chair if you want the visit to be really short. Standing up for a while will probably do you good anyway.

Two more general rules:

Unless there are sound reasons to delay (and that does not mean just because you want to delay) do it now! Don't put off until tomorrow what you can do today. That old adage is absolutely right. Don't lose any of those 960 minutes that comprise today.

Finish one job before starting another. Don't grasshopper around on several jobs. None will get done properly.

Finally:

Include in your plan of work time to think about your next plan of work. Also allow time to think about activities which will increase your overall contribution.

Finding more time

This sounds a bit of a contradiction since we've already been at pains to say there are only 960 available minutes in the day. Of course, you can't find more time in the absolute sense, but you can do three things to make more time for work.

Work Longer Hours?

Within reason, for most people, yes! Try starting work a bit earlier instead of falling through the office door at 9 a.m. Quarter hour, half hour, one hour? Try half an hour for a start. You can easily vary it afterwards. It's amazing what that quiet half hour can do. Use it for the hard tasks when quiet thought and hard concentration are essential.

As well as an early start, what about the other end of the day? A few extra minutes to finish up before the next day can work wonders.

You must decide for yourself how much extra time you either wish to or can work. Some men or women will work all the hours they can in an endeavour to reach the pinnacle of their ambitions. A large number of people like to do extra time in moderation. Extra time does a lot towards work enhancement, but for most people it will be in moderation and the timings varied.

Delegate

Let others do some of the work. There are triple advantages from delegating. You have more time to do your job, and some more delegated from your boss. You are providing training and opportunities for other people. You are preparing yourself for promotion.

One of the enemies of delegation is the apparently logical attitude that it sometimes takes longer to tell someone what to do than it takes to do the job. This is a fatal trap with no escape, for it gets worse on each occasion. Delegate now!

The third way to make more time is much more subtle, much more difficult to achieve, but gives great rewards. It's a tuning up process. *It's more work in the same time.*

There are certain basic aids you can cultivate. Give yourself a week or two to get these aids going for you and think back to what you used to do. Improvements of 20, 30 and 40 per cent or more are common.

Read a lot

In this IT age any manager who does not continue to learn will rapidly lose ground, not only in his own skill, but in his company. Don't let it go: keep up to date. There will be plenty of reading matter about the company, and about relationships with customers and other employees.

In any management job, information about it is probably coming out of publishers in encyclopaedic quantities. You might ask 'How on earth can I be expected to keep up to date with this tremendous volume of information?' First, you will receive only a part of this information. The market is not perfect and you will not know that a lot of it exists. There will still be enough to cause a problem. What has to be done is to read more in less time. Read faster.

Most people still read at the same speed as they did in their last year in full-time education. There are three interesting facts which when combined can show you how to read very much faster with full comprehension:

- During reading the eye and the mind are at work. The ability of the mind to comprehend is very much faster than the usual speed of the eye when reading.
- Slow reading causes the mind to lose attention, although the person is not aware of it happening.
- The usual reading method is word by word first, and then comprehension of the sentence or small paragraph afterwards. This means again that the mind is limited by the speed of the eye movement, which is slowed up to read word by word.

If you were to learn morse code, you would soon find out that to recognize a character by its individual dots and dashes would be impossible above a speed of a very few words per minute. The character must be read as a whole.

While the analogy is not exact, reading faster has the same principle. Read in the units your mind wants, not word by word. First it will be complete sentences, then more. It will take time, but it will work. The reward is:

- Recognizing quickly useless material.
- More knowledge in less time.
- Keeping ahead of the competition.

Don't talk too much

It would be a peculiar existence if nobody talked, but maybe some of us talk too much. While we talk, it's doubtful if we can really concentrate on much else. Don't be taciturn, but be economical in talking. That does not mean be uninteresting, it means just saying what we have to say in a minimum of words. Often it can just be the avoidance of repetition. If you think about talking time when you talk, the economy will follow.

The telephone is a great invention, but also a great tempter. The temptation to go on and on is compelling. Don't be tempted! Don't forget that if you talk unnecessarily three things happen:

The caller is wasting time and money.
The person at the other end is wasting time.

A telephone line is tied up and perhaps stops someone else from communicating important news.

Don't write too much

This is a great area for saving time. Make business letters and memos short and to the point. For example:

Don't write:

'We enclose the form No. 203 which we should be glad if you would kindly sign on the dotted line and return as soon as convenient to you so that we can investigate the claim you are making. If it proves satisfactory we shall be pleased to forward you a cheque in due course.'

Write:

'Please sign and return the enclosed form. Your claim will be investigated quickly and if agreed it will be paid.'

There is no doubt the example could be further improved, but there is no need to go beyond the sensible pruning stage. Going further can make a message too terse or too cold. This is not good for communication in general. If work is put into saving time and effort in writing, there are two important results. First, the time of the person receiving the letter is saved and often the message is less ambiguous. Second, more communication takes place because, say, ten notes can be written instead of five. This assumes that we need to write so many memos anyway. If circumstances permit, an even greater saving can be achieved by not writing the letter or memo. There are too many in all the companies we know. Why not a quick phone call instead?

One amusing story we have read, and which we hasten to add is not firm advice, is about a very senior civil servant. He became frustrated with the amount of paper coming into his in-tray. His practice, therefore, every day was to put half of his incoming mail straight into the out-tray without reading it. He calculated he only got about 10 per cent back for a second go.

Into this subject of writing also comes speed. Whatever is done, if it is done faster then, again, total output must improve. Secretarial assistance and word processing help greatly but, if you handwrite, then practise quicker but legible writing for notetaking and short memos.

Listen often

Do you ever remember at school, college or university being taught to listen? Many other subjects, including reading (but not fast reading!), writing, etc. are regularly taught, yet we spend a great deal of our time listening and have never been taught anything about it. There will be many who will scoff at the suggestion, yet not listening properly is an important reason for bad industrial relations and other situations where there is apparent deadlock. Effective listening is very important and a manager cannot manage without that ability.

As a manager, can you answer the following questions about your staff?

- Do they enjoy their work?
- Do they really know what their job is?
- What do they feel towards the company you both work for?
- Are there things wrong beneath the surface?
- Do you understand what they are telling you? Have you listened properly?

If you are perfect don't read on, but we suspect one of these questions may find a tender spot. It does in most of us. Encourage people to talk. Listen and absorb what they say. Put their point back to them by a question, for example 'I'm going to put in my own words what I think you are saying: please tell me if you agree.'

Complaints and information are not nuisances: they enable the manager to learn what is going on; prevent a smouldering situation and an inevitable blow-up.

When someone talks to you do you:

- Claim you are too busy to listen now but later will be fine?
- Continue to read a memo and say 'OK I'm listening'?
- Think about last night while someone is telling you something?
- Find difficulty in listening because the talker is not quite in your mould or seemingly not as intelligent?

Listen and learn. Listen and improve working relations. Listen and increase productivity.

Meetings

A lot of time is wasted on meetings; probably half of them are not necessary and probably all take twice as long as they need. Multiply this time by all the people who attend, by the number of meetings held in a year and then take the total salary bill. The size of this bill would probably equal the national debt.

This does not, of course, mean that all meetings are useless, but time must be well spent. Make sure that when you attend a meeting, the following rules are obeyed:

- There must be a clear object.
- The people who attend must be capable of dealing with the subject.
- The subject must be within the scope and authority of the meeting.
- The agenda and timing must be designed to ensure a quick successful session.
- Weigh up the chairman in advance. He can make or mar the meeting.

Concentration and effectiveness

In all the work we do, whether it is work for reward, a hobby or social help, the keyword must be concentration. It's all a question of bringing the maximum mental or physical energy to bear at the time on a particular task. It's often not easy at first to know whether enough effort is in fact being concentrated on a task. If an awkward nail has to be hammered and it has to be held to keep it in position, most people will concentrate hard. No prizes for the reason: they might hit their fingers. Perhaps unfortunately, most of our work has no immediate finger pain to prove lack of concentration.

It's easier to recognize lack of concentration than concentration itself. Dreaming while looking out of the office window, listening to the exciting story of what happened to someone last night, the recounting of a television programme, and general gossip in the office. All sorts of distractions destroy the concentration we need to do a job in twenty minutes instead of two hours.

All DIY enthusiasts will surely recognize some of the symptoms in the story of the ardent DIY man. He gets up early with a perfect plan of work. First he will finish papering the ceiling of the room he has been decorating for the last week or two. He will then paint the front door which needs doing badly, and then by about 4 p.m. on the Saturday he will slip out to do some last minute shopping.

What actually happened? He got up at 8.00 a.m., had breakfast by 8.30 a.m. and started papering at 8.40. While papering he noticed that his papering table had a screw missing in one of the hinges. He went off to his shed to get a screw. While there, he remembered he had meant to put a shelf up to hold some flowerpots which were in danger of getting broken on the floor. 'Well that won't take long. I'll do that,' he said. The shelf was up by 9.45. 'Oh that's a relief, now I can get through the shed to my lathe and finish off the chair legs I was shaping.'

Chair legs completed by lunchtime. Into lunch and suddenly he remembered he had started papering. 'Well after lunch I'll soon finish that.' After lunch, hard at work papering, while putting up the next to last piece our friend sees the wall brackets he has recently bought. 'I must see whether they fit.' By 4 p.m. he has fixed two brackets and hears his wife call him to go shopping. The saga goes on and another week has to go by before the ceiling is finished. Lack of concentration? Grasshopping? Lack of planning? Allocation of time?

Education and training

As a manager, you must spare time for education and training – for yourself and your staff. Preparing for work and keeping this preparation up to date is as important for a manager as it is for an athlete to keep in training. Most of us easily recognize the latter's need: not all of us recognize that management and staff have a similar need.

There are many ways to achieve the right education and training and certainly many will be particular to an industry. As far as the manager is concerned, there are several things to do to keep fit in the education and training sense.

- Know the general picture in your trade or profession by belonging to a learned society or trade association. Attend the meetings and read the appropriate literature. This gives you the 'feel' for your work environment. It's dangerous to get isolated in your own job as developments outside move faster than you think. Get to know people in your type of work.

- Look around often at new products, in reality and in literature, to learn what similar industries and other industries are producing.
- Find time to improve your grasp of your own job. Get as deep an understanding of the principles of what you are trying to do as you can. Go on appropriate courses. They can have a double advantage. There is further training and also the chance to meet other people.
- Find time for education. This means education in a general sense. A broadening of knowledge in subjects completely unrelated to your work. History, fine arts; such activities will give you pleasure, relaxation and interest. They will in their subtle way make you even fitter mentally to tackle the daily work flow.

Fitness

It's pretty obvious that if a person is unfit, he or she canot work at a desirable pace to make a real impact on the work situation and use time to the best advantage. Enough sleep and proper food are essential. No one can prescribe the very best solution, for we must each find it for ourselves. It is fairly certain that eating and drinking in moderation are important. If you must smoke, then this should be controlled, as there is little doubt that heavy smoking brings nasty rewards, let alone a lack of fitness. What else do we need? Some fun, some relaxation and forgetting work sometimes, are all essentials to a balanced mind and body.

6 Communicating

What is communication?

We may not often stop and think about the magic and evil of communication. It's magic when it's good, clean and satisfactory to all involved. It's evil when it is used to distort minds, contrary to accepted standards of goodness, cleanliness and decency. Hot wars, cold wars and their aftermath show some of the evils. Away from the evil, however, let's talk about business communication which, although one of its facets may be to alter people's minds from one course of action to another, is still within the ethical environment of a normal business community.

Communication occurs in all our social, business and political lives. As far as business is concerned, if we want value for money, communication must be purposeful. To be effective, we want the response we planned.

Types of communication

Communication in early man was by gestures, grunts and groans ('Has it changed?' we sometimes ask). In what is a very short time in earth history man has progressed through alphabets, printing, telegraph, radio, television, computers, satellites and more. Man's ingenuity in communication seems unbounded.

In human-to-human terms, all methods slot into the basic forms: speaking, writing, gesturing, listening and visual. We have not yet come very close to direct mind-to-mind communication but who can say when? The silent treatment of a strike-breaker or the silence of a boy- or girl-friend after a quarrel are very close to mental communication. You may have heard the much-told story of communication by denial. The story is about the skipper of a boat who put in the ship's log 'The mate was drunk again last night'. The mate, seeing the entry, and determined to get his revenge merely entered in the log 'The captain was sober last night'. The implication was obvious. Advertisements sometimes use this type of implied criticism against others. 'Our powder does not cause rashes, eat your skin away or slowly kill you!'

In communication, gestures are important. If someone has suffered, a comforting arm round the shoulder is often better than too much talk. We all use gestures: the raised eyebrow, the thumbs up, the pointed finger and many others.

Visual communication is big business everywhere, from advertising to business courses. Whole enterprises deal in the art and science of visual presentation. Television is a powerful example.

We shall talk more about writing and speaking, but some words now about the most under-estimated part of communication, listening.

Listening

Intelligent and concentrated listening is vital to business communication. In industrial relations, all parties must listen with the greatest care. We all tend to fall foul of two important problems in listening:

- Firstly, we think we have heard some or all of it before. Immediately the mind registers this belief, the acuteness and concentration of our listening lessens and we may lose a point that was new. The danger is obvious.
- Secondly, the mind, in its search for the real meaning in what is being said, may fix, for various reasons, on an incorrect conclusion. This may be a genuine misunderstanding caused by a garbled message, but could easily be not really wanting to understand.

The question of not really listening nearly always occurs because two parties have quite different interests, or because the scene has been wrongly set by one of the communicators. Listening includes asking questions to clarify points made or the restatement of the issue in your words. This gives the other person a clear check on whether you are reading the same meaning into the communication.

An example of listening in its negative form was told to us by a works manager friend of ours. One of his foremen had told a machine operator 'Clean up your machine, it is dirty and thus dangerous'. The man had resented this and before long they were arguing hammer and tongs about everything bar the dirty machine. They had both adopted attitudes, were not really listening to each other, and were much more interested in simply arguing. The manager happened to hear them and quickly calmed down both people. The problem was really this. The foreman quite rightly was not going to have a dirty machine because dirtiness was often a prelude to danger. It was not just plain 'bull'. Unfortunately, the worker had not been on this particular machine for most of the time and couldn't explain to the foreman that he felt it was a bit unjust. Their points of view could not be reconciled. They were not listening. The foreman should not have persisted in the argument, he would have done better to have listened and found out what the real grievance was.

Effective communication

For a manager the importance of effective communication can hardly be over-emphasised. It is undoubtedly a major task of every manager and directly affects all working relationships.

If a manager cannot communicate properly he cannot possibly hope to get the best out of his own staff or be able to interpret and influence higher management. Another aspect is the effect on his own and his company image every time he writes, telephones or appears in public or at meetings. There is no shortage of reasons for the need to communicate effectively.

In general terms, communication effectiveness depends on how credible the sender is to the receiver, since the receiver usually ascribes a motive to the message:

- The message is more likely to be successful if it supports a belief already held.
- A communication which is repetitive or has a prolonging influence, in that it gives information little by little, is often more effective.
- Short sentences with familiar words and active verbs make a communication interesting and persuasive.

Obstacles

To understand how to communicate properly involves understanding the obstacles, and there is no shortage of these either! One of the biggest obstacles, which also sets the scene for many others, is consciously or unconsciously refusing to see the point of view of the other party. We say consciously as there is no doubt that some people are obstinate from a purely political point of view. Unconsciously refusing to see is very common. To provide a core of ideas or obstacles for you to expand we list some common ones below:

Prejudice   This comes from deep-seated beliefs often stemming from personal experience or the experience of family or close friends. It can also arise from a lack of intelligence or a wish not to learn, in a general sense.

Wrong time or place   This is often unfortunate for a person with a good idea. He seems unable to communicate it to others for many complex, unidentifiable reasons. Yet some short time afterwards, perhaps, the same audience is told the same thing by someone else and action commences straightaway. There is no clever answer to the wrong time or place obstacle, except to try to measure the receptivity before telling all.

Too complex   This is a fairly straightforward obstacle. We must set the level of our communication to suit the audience. If our message is too complex for them they will stop listening with their minds, although they appear to be awake!

Unclear   This does not necessarily mean a mumbled or garbled message, that would be easy to spot. By unclear, we also mean a bad logical composition. It's essential to get a message across to someone in such a way that the listener almost leads himself to the answer by the power of the logic in the message.

Jargon   There is plenty of this about today, and we hope we haven't fallen into the trap by using it somewhere in this book! Jargon is, of course, special language that all industries have appropriate to their industry. In computer language, examples are hardware, software, interface, etc. Don't use such jargon when reporting upwards unless you're quite sure your receiver understands.

Fear   A lot more people than we might realize don't communicate on certain issues because they are fearful of the consequences. They are worried about whether they will look foolish or even worse.

There are many more we might list and it is certainly useful to examine ourselves and the environment in which we work to find obstacles to communication which we can help to remove. A company problem, as distinct from individual, is sometimes the complete lack of a communications policy. There should be one in every company where it is no longer possible for the owner or general manager to talk to everyone at fairly regular intervals. If a policy does not exist then a vacuum forms as far as information is concerned. Such a situation breeds rumours and non-facts faster than any other. If you are in the position to do so, try to ensure that a communications policy exists. This will consist of company instructions, company announcements, department information, suggestion schemes and the like. Probably more important, however, is for your staff to feel *you* keep them informed. There will sometimes be things you cannot tell them, but they want to be kept 'in the picture' and should be as much as possible.

This feeling of 'belonging' is not just a 'good' thing to do for human relations. It can help any company or organization to achieve better results if people get a greater awareness of what is going on. The problem of communication in, say, a large government department is immense. There may be anything from 20 to 100,000 people. Furthermore, a department may be scattered over London in perhaps thirty or forty buildings and indeed in offices anywhere in the United Kingdom. However, without good communication there are many interplays that will not take place and we get the old problem of the left hand not knowing what the right is doing.

This means it is essential to spend money on communication, probably with a senior official in charge, and to supplement this with news-sheets, information circulars and the like. However, once again, the communication foundations will depend upon the way the top managers communicate with one another, and likewise with their subordinates.

Unfortunately, it is also a fact that up to 60 per cent or more of information that ought to be transferred is lost in the filter action of management chains in most large departments and industries.

Communicating with your staff

In talking with your staff there are generally five communication needs:

1 Tell them to do something
2 Tell them about something
3 Listen to their work or personal problems and ask questions to make sure you understand
4 Guide and train them
5 Discuss common problems

In all of these it is necessary for you to contribute as much to successful communication as you can, and that will include time to study the situations. Knowledge of background and personalities helps in the 'listening' part of communication provided the enemy, prejudice, does not enter. The sort of remark calculated to ruin any discussion is to say to a rather hot-tempered person 'You know the trouble with you George is . . . '. Immediately 'George' is on guard, and easy communication may become impossible for some time.

When you tell your staff to do something, it should be done in such a way that the reason for telling is understood, even if the facts are unpleasant. Most people, basically, want to understand, but there are so many communication difficulties about that it may seem sometimes as though they don't.

In communicating with your staff, you will always get more response by leading them to a conclusion rather than by simply telling them. They have to understand, to agree the conclusion is the right one and then say to themselves: 'I've got this message clear. I may not care for the content but I understand it.'

In listening to their work problems, bear in mind that good listening is important to both of you if the job is to proceed in the best manner. How can you instruct, help or guide a man with a problem if you don't understand the problem properly?

If the problem is personal, then sympathetic listening is important, but any advice you may give must clearly be shown to be your personal opinion, not your company's, unless the two are really interwoven, in which case your competence to deal with it must be clear. Certainly, items like purchasing a house or investing can be answered with frankness, but the answer is your opinion, not your guarantee.

Communicating with your manager

First of all, we hope he listens. It can be maddening when the 'boss' never listens. If you find this is so, there may be something you can do about it. Analyse the problem. Is it because he is just that sort of person and, in fact, he doesn't listen to anybody? Is it because you are so uninteresting or long winded or both that he dare not take a chance on listening to you?

A manager wants information in the fastest time, provided it is factual and meaningful. There is so much potential information hanging over his head that if it all fell on him he would not have time to do his job. Keep it short is a good policy.

Keys to success

These are the keys to successful communication with your manager. Be:

- Timely
- Short
- Meaningful
- Factual
- Unambiguous
- Convincing

Timeliness is obviously important. Old information on current problems is usually useless and if quick decisions have to be made the manager wants the relevant information quickly. There will be little thanks for out-of-date information.

If the message is short, the manager is almost bound to read it. If it is long he may put it aside, only skim it, give it to somebody else to read, or find it difficult to get the facts because they are surrounded by irrelevancy. The manager's time is precious. A long message is also more prone to mistakes and wandering off the point. It is worth the effort to get the message short.

Even though short, your information must still be meaningful. Half a message that doesn't answer the question is still useless. The manager may then have to ask again (or ignore you next time) and this takes up more valuable time. The receiver, as he reads your message, should get a clear picture of what you wanted to say.

If what you have to say is not factual, then, unless you are very clear about this point and explain the basis of your hypothesis, your manager will wonder what reliance he may place in you. He will respect facts and the intelligent use of theories stated to be such. Many situations are not easy to express as facts, quickly and conveniently. Judgement must be included, and should be clearly labelled as such. Although most people start off in the belief that the message is true, disbelief and, far worse, disenchantment with the sender will follow quickly.

Ambiguity is a subtle enemy. You write what you think is an excellent, clear message and what does the silly chap who receives it do? He says he cannot understand it: it might mean this or it might mean that. Before you argue with him, be careful. Unless he is deliberately trying to be awkward, *he* probably genuinely does see more than one interpretation and, after all, he is reading it. We must watch ambiguity carefully and try and put ourselves in the reader's place. What possible misconstruction could there be?

The last of our keys to success in communicating with our manager is convincing him that our solution or recommendation is the right one. We hope we are much more than halfway, because we have been careful so far. Now we need the extra push, the final argument to clinch the matter. This is worth some thought as the whole object of communication is to get the desired effect from the message.

We've already said that all managers want to spend their time wisely. With this in mind, what does your manager want to hear? He certainly doesn't want a running commentary on your work or even all your achievements listed. What he does want to hear are reports from you on anticipated deviations from budget, time plans or performance of your agreed work objectives. He will want to know whether these are temporary setbacks and for how long, or whether the original plan is likely to suffer permanently. He will also want to hear of major achievements as these add credibility to both your efforts.

The general rules for effective communication we have already listed, but it is worth trying to submit your information in a way that the manager understands best. This may be in simple written form, or charts or in a diagram. All managers have their own pet preferences. If you can find your manager's preferred method, it will probably save you a lot of time in the future. It takes time to communicate and the sender must help the receiver in order to get the desired response.

7 Decision making

Delegate

Your first decision: delegate! Wherever and whenever you can, delegate decision making to your staff, provided it is within their capabilities and training. Save yourself for the big ones. Guide your staff by all means, encourage them to think their decisions through thoroughly before they act. Educate them in the decision-making processes, but let them make decisions, and the mistakes that will be inevitable, to make them develop.

Define the real problem

A decision demands the need for a decision; a problem or a question must be posed. That seems a bit obvious, but do we understand what that problem or question really is? Most of us, in fact, find it far easier to answer questions that were never asked. Our favourite example of this is the committee. A committee meets nominally to discuss what appears to be a simple issue. Without even trying, the meeting drifts off into philosophical questions which probably have no answer, but on such occasions we're all such jolly good philosophers and poor decision makers.

First reveal the question that is being asked: stark, clear, naked, stripped of all frills.

After we have revealed the question, we must ask ourselves: 'Is this the right question?'

In a company making electronic measuring equipment there was continuous trouble with the power supply unit. Despite much communication with the sub-contractor who made the units, there was no improvement. A case was put up to make the supplies in the factory from parts made by various outside contractors. Factory loading was such that total in-house manufacture was not possible. The director whose job it was to resolve the decision first defined the problem:

- The power supplies were troublesome.
- The present factory loading was heavy.
- It was certain that in-house assembly from bought-in parts would be better.

He then asked himself a further question.

As the power supplies had proved very troublesome, why not make them completely and off-load other less critical work to sub-contractors.

The information after investigation was revealing. By asking the right questions, it was found that off-loading some simple electronic assemblies made room for the more critical power supply.

Whose responsibility?

By this stage, not only should the real question have been asked but also the appropriate level identified for decision. You will learn whether you can make your own decision on a particular issue and get on with it, or whether you will have to pass the problem up the line to more senior management. It is just as bad to make a decision for which you do not have either competence or authority, as it is to fail to make a decision which you do have competence and authority to make.

Is it our problem?

The next stage is to ask yourself whether the problem comes within the scope of the business. Perhaps the problem has nothing to do with the business or it is beyond the capabilities of the company and staff to solve. In other words, is it an unreal question? Have we strayed into 'Walter Mitty' land in trying to tackle such problems?

It is surprising how many businesses fall into the trap of tendering for a contract which, if accepted, would place them in jeopardy. This is because they have neither the experience, finance nor manpower to carry out the contract satisfactorily.

The decision-making process

The possession of a decision making process, valuable as it is, cannot provide the whole key to success. There are no certain mysterious management mathematics that can bring a decision out of an equation. Decision making needs a system; it needs management techniques to help define the problem and show trends, but it also needs practice and a willingness to accept carefully calculated risks.

Problems are of two basic kinds:

1 Those where the question contains the answer
2 Those which require the whole process of decision making

An example of the first kind, and some would say of everyday management action, concerns a wholesaling firm. The manager, looking at the summarized list of orders obtained from his microcomputer, notices that orders are severely down from one of his better customers. The initial decision is clear. He asks the question: Why? He finds that the customer has received late deliveries and that quality was bad in a batch of imported footballs. The manager sees the customer, arranges for the exchange of all goods in that batch and assures him that such occurrences are very rare. The customer apparently is satisfied.

The other problems are not so easy; they require the whole armoury of decision making. They require practice in dealing with them, systematically working through the process of decision making. Many people know a lot of things about management from experience, but some will never succeed because they cannot put the process together. 'Practice makes perfect' is still a good adage. A famous golfer was told by an onlooker 'That was a lucky shot'. The golfer replied 'Yes, and the more I practice, the luckier I get'.

Analyse the problem

Timing

One of the first actions should be to determine when the decision must be made. This dictates how long you can wait before making a decision. It may be too early for the decision, in which case you may take more time on the problem if it appears to warrant it. As you look at the problem it may become obvious that it is already

77

too late to make any useful decisions at all. Unnecessarily hurried decisions can be just as dangerous as decisions that are too late. However, if you diagnose that the decision is urgent, then take the decision, if it is in your province to do so, after you have carried out the minimum necessary checks. Remember Montrose's famous lines:

> He either fears his fate too much,
> Or his deserts are small,
> Who durst not put it to the touch
> To win or lose it all.

Assessment of risk

In every decision there is an element of risk. All decisions involve some judgement and the future is an uncharted jungle. Judgement and future equals risk. We must try to gauge that risk in money or people terms, against the reward that may also stem from the decision. Whether we can ever have a neat balance sheet in quantified terms is debatable, but we should at least be able to write down the pros and cons and make our judgements on that basis.

Critical factors and fact finding

If you can find the key factor early in your search for facts you may save a lot of time and money. Suppose you have to decide whether to proceed to the experimental stage with a new domestic tape recorder. It is going to play longer and with greater quality than any model on the market. It also has to be very small in size. You get all the facts from your company, there are no technological problems, no manufacturing problems and it looks all set.

You look at the project to see what is the item least under your control: the magnetic tape. You have it checked again and find that it would have to be specially made at an exorbitant cost. You stop the project; you make a decision that will save your company money. If you think that the problem was so obvious that nobody would actually get that far, you would be wrong. Some companies have gone up the wrong road with their pet projects and lost a lot of money. It happens almost daily because of insufficient analysis.

Take another, totally different case that we know about. A small village shop changed ownership and the new owner found that by good marketing in the shop he raised his turnover by 40 per cent.

78

He added new lines to grocery, stationery and allied lines. The business continued to develop. There was no hardware shop in the village so he spent several hundred pounds on additional space next to his existing shop and packed it with hardware, paints and other similar goods. The turnover from this side of the business was abysmal. He wondered where he had gone wrong. Everything else sold all right, so why not the paints, etc.? The answer, when he really analysed the problem, was not difficult. The women of the village liked to shop there for groceries and other basic items; bus service was bad to the town and he was fairly competitive in his prices in any case. When it came to hardware and paints, however, the men went to the town where a very large hardware and builders' merchants store was situated. The village store could not compete as a side-line business.

Develop more than one answer

Case 1

The chairman of a large furniture makers confided to us one of his problems in the timing of decisions and assessment of risks. All the estimates and predictions he could get from his experts, together with current selling figures, indicated some downturn in the volume of trade. It looked as though the decision he might have to make would be to shut down one of his smaller factories and make staff redundant. Was this the right time for this decision? Because the savings from such a move would take time to come into effect, it was no good waiting until the trade had declined to a point where his profits were declining faster than they should be. If the trade was really going to decline, due, perhaps, to various government measures and other reasons, he must act. The chairman decided to look at the question again from the viewpoint of a completely alternative course of action.

Fortunately the company was not short of liquid assets and a possible alternative course was found. Another company manufacturing for the export trade, and which had a good order book, was not able to take full advantage of this because of lack of working capital. An amicable agreement was reached between the two firms and the new combine was able to meet all the export orders.

Case 2

This is not a happy one. Mr H was employed as a production engineer, but after some years in this work decided to start his own business. The reasons were as follows:

- He had two sons, one 19 and one 22. Both were in semi-skilled engineering jobs. Mr H thought he and his two sons could work in the business. (Mistake number one: he never asked his sons what they thought.)
- Some months earlier he had been told by a motor mower company that if ever he decided to go into business they could give him work. (Mistake number two: Mr H did not research his market and his cashflow prospects.)
- He thought his savings of £9000 would be sufficient until he began to make money. (Mistake number three: no proper cashflow estimates.)

Mr H ordered the necessary machinery and spoke enthusiastically to his two sons. Neither was the least bit interested.

Mr H started manufacture in his double garage. After some months it became apparent that insufficient money was being made and the balance of his savings was reducing.

Mr H then did rather well. He went out and obtained some more business from another firm which gave him the extra income he wanted. This went on quite well for two more years. He was then told by the second firm that his prices were too high. Mr H decided to buy more machinery on borrowed money. (Mistake number four: again the same error of not researching the market.) Sad to say, by the time the machinery was in, the firm had gone elsewhere and, with the recession biting, Mr H found things very lean indeed. He eventually had to sell up at a considerable loss. His decision-making processes were poor. His biggest mistakes were:

- Simply not going through an ordered decision-making process.
- Pursuing a false hope of 'a family business'.
- Having no cashflow plan.
- Reliance upon a tiny customer base – no marketing plan.

Mr H would have been better off salvaging what he could before he got more deeply into debt, or more actively seeking work for his original machinery. Mr H did get another job and is still paying his debts!

Search for alternatives

We must, then, always look for alternatives in our decision-making process, as there may be a totally different way of solving a particular problem from that first envisaged. We must keep an open mind to receive all the information on the possibilities that may exist. One of the biggest dangers is the 'flywheel' decision; a decision based on the flywheel of the past, like not stopping a loss-making operation in time. Some questions seem to demand just one answer and the danger is simply to agree. Equally, a hasty, badly thought out decision could be worse than leaving the decision a bit longer. There invariably are alternatives. They have to be found.

Making the decision

The steps to the decision are these:

- Understand the problem.
- Make sure you have the right question.
- Assess whether it is your responsibility to make the decision.
- Check whether the question is valid.
- Look at the timing needed for the decision.
- Assess the risks.
- See what alternatives exist.
- Search for critical factors.

You are now ready to make the decision and how you make it is important. The content of what you say must accurately reflect what you want to say. Too often good decisions have been marred by poor explanations. The people who receive the decision must know what to do without doubt, particularly if the decision is an urgent one. We say more about clarity and non-ambiguity in the chapter on communications.

It is important when you make the decision to know who you must tell; there may be a series of people who, unless you tell all of them, cannot properly implement your decision. You must have planned in advance how to deal with any effects of your decision. It may be necessary in some cases to accompany your decision with explanations and answers to probable questions that may arise. What we are doing is to make sure that our decision is clear and final. A story told to us by a builder friend illustrates what can happen if decisions are not made properly.

81

The chief contracts manager issued an instruction to his contract managers on various sites:

'To improve our costing accuracy per site and to give you (the site manager) more information about site profit, you will personally check all invoices before we pass them for payment.'

In essence this was a sensible request, but unfortunately the decision had not been thought about deeply enough and the questions soon started to roll in:

'Have I got to come down to the office, it's about a hundred miles you know?'
'Are you going to post them?'
'How do I know when you've got invoices?'
'What about the advice notes, will they do?'

In fact, nobody really knew how to deal with what seemed a simple enough decision and request. The next decision was: 'We will post them to the sites.' This started off and the first realization of trouble was when a supplier cut off supplies at one site because the account, due weekly, had not been paid. An examination showed that invoices were now being held up in transit and checking, etc. for well over a week. A further decision was made: 'We will send a copy invoice to the sites.' Unfortunately this could not prevent some invoices being paid at Head Office before anyone knew whether they were correct as to deliveries to the site. The situation was in a muddle. It was a good idea in the first place, but was not thought out properly before the decision was made. What happened in fact was that copies went out for a while and the scheme was then dropped. The company went back to their previous system. About six months later another attempt was made to tighten up the system: this time it was thought out more thoroughly; simple changes were made to the sites' paperwork system and delivery returns sent in with other papers that had to come in regularly.

Action check

After the communication of the decision comes the action check. Has the decision been received correctly and implemented? In an imperfect world there will always be some who do not give the decision clearly, and some who do not receive it clearly. Action may be put in hand which is not relevant or even harmful. To be aware of this is to be able to guard against it and thus reduce the failures to an insignificant level. If more than one level of management is involved, then the greater the risk of error. Checking is not easy. Managers cannot walk around regularly visiting staff two or three levels down and saying 'Did my manager pass on my decision correctly?'

The checking actually starts with the choice of management and the taking of great care in communicating decisions. Checking is made easier if the decision is stated as clearly as possible and not in some peculiar bureaucratic language. If the decision warrants it, then it should be written and circulated to all concerned. It is clear that communication and decisions go hand in hand, and one can easily destroy the other.

In checking and monitoring the action and results, there must be a readiness to adjust where necessary. 'Where necessary' is another decision process with practical inputs of results so far. Conversely, adjustments should not be made until a proper time has elapsed. Like a ship's rudder, over-steering can have inconvenient consequences.

8 Negotiating

Everybody negotiates

Every manager is a negotiator. He negotiates with his staff and his own boss, although he may not always recognize these discussions as negotiations. In a large company he may be responsible for negotiating with other departments. He may also be responsible for negotiating on behalf of his firm, with customers, suppliers, public authorities and other bodies.

Responsibilities

Depending upon your position in your firm, your negotiating responsibilities could include:

- Building alterations
- Staff grievances
- Customer complaints
- Special deals with customers or suppliers
- A joint venture with another firm
- Securing government or local government assistance
- Allocation of car park space
- Many others

The more senior you become, the more time you spend in negotiation. The broader your function, the wider the range of negotiations you will undertake. The manager of an independent retail shop, which is not part of a chain, will have to negotiate over a whole range of matters, while the departmental manager in a large firm employing thousands of staff may only negotiate over a very narrow range of issues.

Whatever your job as a manager, there are a few simple rules to follow in negotiation. Follow them and you will improve your performance.

Define your objective

It is obvious that you are unlikely to succeed in negotiation unless you know what you want. Deciding on what you want may not be so simple. There may be a wide range of outcomes of a negotiation, ranging from the ideal to the just acceptable. For instance, in negotiating for a new office building you may want car parking space for thirty staff cars and a dozen visitors' cars, as well as access for a delivery van three times a day. The bare essentials may be access for the delivery van plus four parking spaces for visitors. You could settle for this, but you will use your skill as a negotiator to come closer to the ideal.

Am I the right person?

Having defined what it is that you wish to negotiate about and what your objectives are, ask yourself: 'Am I the right person to negotiate?'; 'Do I have the right knowledge, experience, and authority to negotiate on this subject?'; 'Will I be an acceptable negotiator to the other party?'. This is not a time for undue modesty. It is necessary to answer the questions objectively. If the subject to be negotiated will involve specialist knowledge of a commercial, financial, or technical nature, you may not be the right person. If the negotiation will involve a decision, which you are not authorized to make, the negotiation should be conducted by the person who does have the authority. Alternatively, he should be persuaded to define the limits within which he authorizes you to negotiate.

Choosing your opposite number

Some people, particularly those with a sales background, always go for the top man. This may not be right. The chief executive of a multinational corporation will not negotiate the purchase of pencils or the sale of waste paper from his computer department. If you want to secure a development grant from the Department of Trade and Industry, you are more likely to succeed if you start with the right middle-grade civil servant rather than the Minister or Permanent Under-Secretary. If you want a modification made to an elaborate piece of electronic equipment, you may be wise to negotiate with the specialist who understands the problem, rather than with his managing director.

Be sure that you understand the extent of the other party's authority to negotiate. It is one thing to negotiate with a person who has full authority to settle on the spot. It is entirely different if you are negotiating with a person who merely has authority to recommend to a committee, a board, or even just to a more senior executive. It is irritating to reach the end of a lengthy and difficult negotiation, when you believe that your last concession has won over the other party, only to be told that the proposed agreement will be recommended. This leaves the other party with the option to come back later to reopen negotiations.

The meeting place

The next choice is the place and circumstances for the negotiating meeting. There are implications in choosing to negotiate on his ground, your own ground, or on neutral ground. It may be helpful for you to make the other party come to you, so that you are in familiar surroundings with your supporting staff on call. It may be more helpful to meet in his office, where you can obtain a first-hand feel for his position and organization. In some cases the other party may appear to give you little option but to meet him on his home ground. If you feel it really is essential to hold the meeting away from the other party's premises, you should be able to manage this with a little ingenuity. There may, of course, be good reasons for wanting a meeting on neutral ground. Secrecy may be important. You may not wish staff to know in advance that you are considering the possibility of contracting out work that is presently being done in-house, or that you are trying to sell some of your premises. In the extreme, you would not want news of a merger or takeover to leak out prematurely.

Privacy

Wherever you choose to meet, you require privacy and no interruptions for the planned negotiation period. Trying to negotiate in an office where there are frequent interruptions is unsatisfactory. It breaks the train of thought and can result in the other party becoming impatient and dismissive of your point of view. Some planned interruptions may be helpful. Appropriate refreshment at the start of a meeting helps to put the parties at ease. In the course of a long negotiation, discreetly served refreshments throughout the day can help to keep the negotiation flowing smoothly.

The businessman's lunch is notorious as a setting for business negotiations. There may well be times when lunch or dinner is an appropriate setting for a negotiation, when some fairly simple point needs to be made or agreed with a politician, civil servant, or senior executive. In the majority of cases, however, particularly at the departmental manager level, negotiations are best carried out in the office or conference room. Meals can, of course, play their part in a protracted sales negotiation as part of the information-gathering and softening-up process.

Listen

Listen to the other party. There is always a temptation to press your argument and to put it as fully and clearly as possible. This is necessary, but it is even more important to listen to what the other party says. His comments may indicate that you have not identified his key interest correctly. They may indicate that he has a particular sticking point that you had not anticipated – something that must be added to or removed from your proposition if it is to stand any hope of agreement. Something that he says may open up a fresh avenue of negotiation by indicating the importance of some aspect that you had overlooked. Nor is it just what he says which you should follow. Not every negotiator is an experienced poker player. Watch his face and particularly his eyes for the impact of what is said. Note what he smiles at and what he frowns at. If he is accompanied by advisers, note his reactions to what they say. Which of them seems to influence him most?

Be careful as you listen. It is not sufficient to hear what the other party says. You need to understand what he means. This is particularly important when dealing with people from a different part of the world. You may think that you speak the same language as an American, Australian, or Canadian. You don't. Words and phrases have different meanings. In particular, the use of jargon and slang can lead to misunderstanding. To a lesser extent, a Yorkshireman and a Londoner may use words differently. Jargon words such as 'compatible', 'protocol', and 'multiplexor' may be given different meanings by people in different industries – and sometimes even by people in the same industry.

87

Both sides must win

In any successful negotiation both sides must win. In business life, unconditional surrender is rarely a satisfactory outcome to a negotiation. You want the other party to feel that he has derived something of value from the negotiations so that he will feel as committed as you do to the implementation of any agreement that is reached. This means that you have to do your homework before the negotiation and also be perceptive during the negotiations themselves.

Why is the other party interested? What does he want from the negotiation? What is the key benefit that would attract him? The answer to these questions is not always simple. Many influences may be at work including the internal politics of the other organization. You will want to angle your case to appeal to the key interest of the other negotiator. Given careful preparation, this can enable you to present a successful case, even when the cards appear to be stacked against you. For instance, suppose a salesman is trying to sell a major capital item to a senior executive. After months of negotiation, it is clear that price is the key issue, and the salesman's price is 20 per cent higher than his main competitor. Maybe he can shift the emphasis from price to total cost of ownership – his equipment may require less people to operate it, or it may require less space, or maintenance costs may be lower, or it may have a longer expected useful life-span. All these factors can be expressed in a price – or total cost of ownership figure. Similarly he might seek to present the price in a more favourable light by quoting a leasing or rental price. For an important contract, he might seek to manipulate the price so that the initial price was as low as possible while recoveries from later charges carried a higher level of profit, for example from the price of spares, licence fees, or maintenance charges. Many salesmen will argue within their firm that they should be allowed to cut the price for the sake of the follow-on business which is certain to come. Not altogether surprisingly, such a concession usually establishes a precedent and permanently reduces the profit margin on business with that customer.

In fact, as most good negotiators realize, price is rarely as important in any negotiation as the raw salesman believes. This is true even when negotiating with a government organization bound to accept the lowest tender, or with a trade union negotiator committed to obtaining the best possible wages for his members. The other party may be more concerned in reality with security. Will you be able to deliver what you promise? Will you wriggle all the way through the agreement using every escape clause and loophole in the small print and take every opportunity to increase costs and delay? Will you let him down personally so that he is seen within his own organization to have failed? Will your firm continue in business? If the agreement requires a degree of skill and knowledge for him to fulfil his part of it, can you be relied upon to guide and help him to cover any of his inadequacies? Has he some problem that could be solved as a by-product of the negotiation? We don't mean that you should indulge in corrupt practices such as paying off the mortgage on his private house. However, he may have a problem such as how to secure immediate delivery of an item he should have ordered six months ago and which is on at least six months delivery lead time from all suppliers. An offer to include this item in the agreement for immediate delivery could be the crucial factor in securing a satisfactory outcome to the negotiation.

The key point is to do your homework thoroughly. Enter the final negotiating session (maybe the only session) knowing not only what you want but also what the other party wants. In doing your homework do not draw the boundaries too tightly.

Be honest

In reality, the majority of negotiations conducted by junior and middle managers are not one-offs. You will have to negotiate with the same people over similar matters repeatedly over the months and years. If you mishandle a negotiation, this can affect your performance over the years. It does not matter if you earn a reputation for driving a hard bargain or for being a shrewd negotiator. It does matter and will seriously damage your prospects if you earn a reputation for negotiating dishonestly. Be honest and open with the other party. Don't tell him you can deliver in three months if you know that it is impossible to deliver in less than six months. Don't say that your access requirements are minimal if you will have half a dozen juggernauts unloading every day.

Words can mean different things to different people. If there is any doubt in your mind as to the other party's meaning make sure that the matter is fully discussed and clarified.

In summary, for a successful negotiation make sure that:

- You are the right negotiator.
- You negotiate with the right person.
- You have a clear aim.
- You understand what the other party wants.
- The meeting place is suitable.
- You listen and understand.
- You offer only what you can deliver.
- The outcome provides benefits for both parties.

Above all, build up your reputation as someone who is an honest and reliable negotiator – a man of your word.

PART 3

Managing your people

9 Setting your people free

Management is people

Management is people. Being a manager is different. It is different because you do your work through the minds and hands of other people. The art of the manager lies in getting other people to work effectively to achieve objectives.

Some people have been managing others since the dawn of history. There have always been those who believed in the Brute Force (BF) and Bloody Ignorance (BI) approach. The 'managers' of Phoenician galleys chained slaves to the oars and employed foremen with whips to stand over them to make sure they pulled together. In its time this was a sound enough system of management. The social climate of the time permitted it and for the slaves there was no acceptable alternative available.

Slavery disappeared gradually throughout the world, but the BF and BI managers still had powerful sanctions to hand. Chief of these was the right to sack without question and at the same time to blacken a man or woman's reputation; in other words to keep employees in fear that they and their families would starve if they did not toe the line. At one time a whole range of fines and other punishments was also available to the manager.

There have always been a few managers who have taken a more enlightened view. This number increased rapidly in the sixties and seventies, spurred on by a social climate which was no longer conducive to the success of BF and BI methods.

The modern management setting

Most advanced industrial countries try to operate their economies at such a level that the majority of the working population are in employment. Heavy unemployment arises from time to time. Much of it is because people are unwilling or unable to move home or change their occupation. Others are virtually unemployable while some are unemployed for relatively short periods while changing jobs. However, there are few industrial countries where a man's family will starve if he is out of work. So far from employers being able to use the sack as a sanction, most managers are far more concerned about how to retain existing staff and how to fill vacancies with competent and effective staff.

As well as the change in the social climate, there has been a major change in the nature of work. This was very gradual in the twenties and thirties but by the sixties and seventies change was rapid.

A hundred years ago only a very few people worked with their minds. The majority were labourers, with a few skilled craftsmen who learned their craft in their teens and practised it throughout the rest of their lives. The number of office workers was a tiny fraction of the number who fill the offices of modern commercial and industrial enterprises. Today the situation has changed and is still rapidly changing. Automation and the introduction of computers have reduced the number of routine non-thinking jobs. The increasing pace of change has resulted in people being more willing to change not just their jobs, but also their trade or profession, as they seek out the opportunities to improve their lot. Many people look forward quite happily to the idea of working in two or three entirely unrelated fields in the course of their working lifetime.

All this has a considerable impact on how successful managers manage people. People no longer work without thought. They are no longer willing to do something merely because they are told to do so. A good manager does not expect them to do so.

In this modern world, you, the manager, must create a climate in which your people bring their minds to work with them and really apply themselves to their jobs.

People do know their jobs

It is quite common when doing systems studies prior to the introduction of a computer system to find that a manager will give you a description of how his system works. The experienced systems man then spends some time with the people who do the work. In most cases the real system is very different from the one described by the manager. Not only different, but better. It is better

94

because it has come to terms with realities. It deals with the exceptions and inconsistencies. It cuts the corners and sorts out the real priorities. We should not be too surprised that the person who is closest to a job, who is actually doing it, has the best knowledge of how it is done. This is as true of a factory job as it is of an office job. The person who knows the job and is interested in it quickly appreciates the effects which change will have on the job. He will know how the job can be improved and done more efficiently to the firm's advantage. He will also know whether the changes are likely to benefit him by making his day's work easier, more interesting or more profitable. How far this knowledge will be applied to the firm's benefit will depend to a great extent on the person's attitude to the firm and his relationship with his manager.

Some managers are extraordinarily successful simply because they listen to what their people have to say and then make use of their ideas. There are those who explain the success of consultants by saying that they go into a firm, listen to everyone and then make a report serving up the best ideas that have come from the people they have spoken to, all at a fee of about £300 a day. It is much cheaper and more effective for managers to listen to their own staff.

So how do we set about the problem of enlisting the interests and energies of people for the benefit of their jobs and the organization for which they work? The first point is to remember that people are human; they are not machines. They are likely to have their fair share of human failings as well as virtues. On the whole, people respond to trust being placed in them. Lack of trust often poses a challenge to people. For instance, in an organization which has a very strict control over timekeeping there is likely to exist an unspoken challenge to outwit the system and arrive half an hour late each day without the system detecting the fact. Similarly, most restrictive rules will provoke opposition and will lead to an enormous waste of time as people try to circumvent the system. Rules must be kept to a minimum and people's energies harnessed positively to produce effective work.

Specifying the job

It may seem obvious to say that the first necessity is that people should know what they are required to do and why. A person who

95

does not know what to do cannot perform at all. In all but the manual or routine jobs a person who does not know 'why' will not perform effectively. To give of their best performance the people who work for you, your people, must have a clear idea of what you expect from them. It is not sufficient that they have a list of tasks to be performed. This may be sufficient for someone who is being used as a mere replacement for horsepower. It is not good enough where you expect people to devote their minds and intelligence, their imagination and creative abilities to the furtherance of your objectives. Such cases are the cases which occur in modern industry and commerce. For these people, the modern 'knowledge' workers, you must make your aims clear and enlist their sympathy and determination to achieve those aims.

In preparing your people for their jobs, the first thing, therefore, is to make sure that they understand what you are setting out to achieve. Next, they must know clearly their own purpose, the part which they must play in achieving the aim. It is highly desirable that you spell out the major tasks which you require them to perform as part of that purpose. Finally, they must know to whom they are responsible, whether to you or to someone else.

In a tight-knit group, working closely together, it may be possible for this all to be done by word of mouth, particularly in a rapidly changing situation. In most normal circumstances it is usual to put this job description in writing. Great care must be taken over the wording of the 'purpose'. The whole job description should be discussed with the person concerned, to make quite sure that he understands the same things from it that you do. In fact, after an initial discussion of the job, it is quite a good idea to make each of your people write the first draft of their own job description. It can then be refined in discussion with them. In this way it should be possible to obtain their complete understanding of what is required and a commitment to doing it.

Apart from the job description it must be clear to each person when you want to hear from them and what. Ideally you will want them to report their progress on some basis, probably routine confirmation that all is going well, according to plan, with exceptions stated and a statement of how they will be put right. Reports may be a set of figures, quantifying performance. In this case they must be figures which really are meaningful to you and which will throw up evidence of things going wrong long before they reach the desperate stage. The object of such reporting is to enable you to control the work for which you are responsible. The report should come naturally out of the needs of the work of your subordinates and should not be a great additional load super-imposed on their normal workload and irrelevant to it.

The whole aim of your job descriptions and your reporting system is to harness the abilities of your people to the job in question and to give them as free a hand as possible to make the greatest contribution they can. You must not be restrictive in the job description. The object is not to stifle the drive and imagination of your people, but rather to encourage them to seek out, recognize and exploit their opportunities for the benefit of the organization.

People are human

Getting a person's job clearly specified and understood is only the first step towards harnessing the whole person and all his or her energy to the job. The good effects of a clearly understood job specification can very quickly be destroyed if your subsequent actions appear to contradict the trust and spirit of partnership implied in the specification. Your attitude to the person must be consistent.

There is an old adage that you should 'do unto others as you would be done by'. In other words, don't complain that your boss is always interfering and won't leave you in peace to get on with the job, and then go and do the same thing with your own staff.

The people who work for you are human beings the same as you are. Some of their interests will not be the same as yours, but their basic humanity is the same. They have the same human aspirations and fears as you do. Treat the people who work for you with normal politeness and courtesy. If you really feel you must be overbearing and rude, try it out on your boss instead, since he won't have to put up with it. If you behave like a pig with your staff, their resentment will be real even if it is hidden. People who feel resentful do not give of their best.

Most people are fearful of the unknown, hence the considerable opposition to change. The mere suspicion that change is coming, for instance after a takeover, may cause fear and a consequent reduction in efficiency. A basic rule for all managers is, therefore, 'Always keep your people in the picture.' People should always be consulted about changes, from the very earliest stages. This is important for two reasons. First, they may contribute ideas which will lead to the change being more effective. Second, the consultation, before a firm plan has been established, is an act of consideration which lets people feel that they can influence the plan. It is not being dictated to them. They can see it evolve, make their contribution, and hopefully see it as a logical outcome of the situation which exists.

Loyalty is two-way

We shall, in the next chapter, consider how people's performance should be measured and how they can be encouraged to improve. There is, however, one other essential factor in setting people free to perform. They must believe that you will look after their interests. It is of the utmost importance that you deal fairly and honestly with your people, and that they should see that this is the case. On no account must you knuckle under to a 'personnel ruling' or to a higher management decision which is unjust in its impact on your people. Loyalty is a two-way matter. You cannot expect loyalty from your people if you are not loyal to them. You must be prepared to fight for your staff.

10 Rewarding and disciplining

We have talked about setting people free to perform. If they do perform well, they should be rewarded for their performance. If a good performance is to be kept up, people should know that their performance is being assessed in some systematic fashion and that, when that assessment justifies it, they will be suitably rewarded.

Performance review

The tools used for this assessment are the performance review and the appraisal interview. The aims of the review form and the associated appraisal interview are:

1   To look systematically at how a person has performed in relation to the objectives set for the period under review (generally a year).
2   To show the person how his manager views his performance.
3   To let the person give his own views on his performance and on his career ambitions.
4   To record the manager's opinion of how the person should be employed in the future.
5   To identify the person's needs for training and development in relation to his performance, his ambitions and his future planned employment.

The completed review also provides a basis on which to decide what reward the person should be given for the period under review.

The review form

This should give the normal administrative details: name, job, age, place of employment, length of time in present job and in the company. This should be followed by a restatement of the job purpose, taken from the person's job description.

The meat of the form comes in a statement of the objectives which the person had to achieve during the year and an assessment of how well or how badly he had performed. If there are valid factors affecting the performance, these should be mentioned. This should be followed by space for comments on any obstacles to the person's better performance, and for comments on his career ambitions and training needs. This may be followed by a summary of the performance assessment and space for the person to sign that he has read and understood the review. There should be space for any confidential comments by the appraiser, including suggestions for promotion or alternative employment, followed by his signature. Finally, there should be space for the appraising manager's manager to comment. A good review form has a minimum of detailed headings and a maximum of space for writing comments.

It is quite a sound plan to have an action form on which to list all the actions agreed at the appraisal interview. This can act as a reminder for both manager and subordinate.

The review procedure

A week or so before the appraisal interview is to take place, the man should be told that his performance is to be reviewed and an appointment should be made. He should at this stage be told briefly the purpose of the review, shown a blank copy of the review form, and possibly given some explanatory notes setting out the purpose of the review, with a reminder that he should sort out his own ideas on the following before the appraisal interview:

1 His job description.
2 His own ideas on how he has performed against the objectives set.
3 Any special success or failure during the year.
4 What help he needs to improve performance.
5 What he thinks he himself can do to improve his performance.
6 How he sees his future career.
7 The sort of training he feels would help him to perform better in his current job and forward his career.

Preparing for the appraisal interview

The manager must make some preparations for the interview. As with any staff interview, he must arrange to hold the interview in an office without interruptions. He should look out the person's job specification and check it over. He should also pencil in draft replies to the questions in the review form to guide him in the appraisal interview.

The appraisal interview

The appraisal interview should open with a restatement of the aims of the interview. The manager should emphasize the need for participation from the person being appraised and try to encourage a free and frank exchange. As the interview proceeds, each question on the form should be discussed, after which the manager writes down his answer. The person should see what is written. It is probably helpful to give him a blank copy of the form to have in front of him during the interview. Finally, at the end of the interview, the man should be handed a copy of the form to read and sign. He may, even after discussion, not agree with your assessment of his performance. In a good review system there will be a procedure for appeal. If this is so in your company, you should explain the appeal system to him. At this stage the agreed actions should be listed separately with a note of whether the action lies on the subordinate or on the manager. Some indication of the timescale for action should also be given. A copy of the action list should be given to the subordinate, preferably there and then, but, if this is not possible, as soon as a copy can be made. The interview should then be closed. Performance review and appraisal systems are time-consuming, but organizations which have used them for some time generally agree that the time and effort is more than repaid in better performance.

It has been traditional in many annual reporting systems to concentrate on aspects of character and potential. We believe that what a manager is concerned with is whether or not his people are performing satisfactorily in their jobs. The fact that a man has deserted his wife, gets drunk every Saturday night or plays rugger for a good club is totally irrelevant unless it affects his performance in his job. Our prime purpose is to measure and then to reward a person's performance against agreed objectives. The whole review and appraisal system must be simple enough for everyone concerned with it to understand what it is all about and for ordinary line managers to operate it as part of their job without having a personnel manager permanently in attendance to explain its ramifications.

The fact that you have an annual appraisal system does not mean that you do nothing about your people's performance during the rest of the year. You are, of course, always concerned about it. If you notice particularly effective work, you should comment on it at the time. Similarly, if someone is performing badly, you should discuss the matter with him and try to agree what action is needed to pull performance back up to standard.

Rewarding

Good performance against objectives set and agreed must be rewarded. There is nothing more stultifying to effort than a situation where a man knows that his salary increase for the year will bear no relation whatsoever to his performance to date. Such a situation is, however, commonplace for government service where strict pay scales exist. Civil servants have to be able to take a longer view and be content with reward by promotion or by the honours system.

To obtain good morale in a workforce and to produce the best performance from people, it is essential that reward be related to performance. A mediocre or poor performance must not in any circumstances be rewarded. Indeed poor performance must be succeeded by satisfactory performance within a limited time or the poor performer must be removed from his job. The rot can spread outwards quite quickly when someone who can plainly be seen not to be performing is not only not penalized but is seen to be as well rewarded as someone whose performance is wholly up to expectations.

In saying this we do not mean to imply that every mistake must be used to condemn the person who made it. We all make mistakes. One of the best ways of learning is from our mistakes. The person who never makes a mistake is one who is dead sure of his facts before he acts and never takes a risk. He is never likely to go very far or achieve very much. We can learn from our mistakes, and we can improve our judgement and our performance by doing so. So don't be too hard on your people just because they make mistakes, provided they recognize that they have made a mistake, why they have made it, and don't make the same mistake twice. Anyone can make a mistake once; only a fool makes the same mistake twice.

Disciplining

Poor performance cannot be tolerated and certainly must not be rewarded. Yet this does not mean we should be inhuman. Poor performance may be due to a number of reasons. It may be our fault for giving someone a job for which he is not suitable. We must not penalize him for our own failure. He may have been promoted to that level at which he performs incompetently. If this sounds unconvincing, read *The Peter Principle* (see Bibliography). It is also possible that a period of rapid change has left a man far behind. This is a particularly difficult case, as it frequently happens to people who have given long and loyal service to an organization, but who are no longer able to adapt to a period of rapid change. Their lack of performance in their current job cannot be tolerated, yet it would be callous to throw them on the dole queue after the company has had their services in their more productive years. A real attempt must be made to find a job for them where their strengths and abilities can be used productively. When someone is falling down on the job, it is easy to overlook his strengths and abilities. Yet they exist in all of us and it is certain that they exist in people who have served your company well for many years. If there has been a real decline in capability with premature onset of old age or some other cause which makes them unsuitable for any productive job in the company, then they will have to go. They should in these circumstances be treated generously, both as to pension and a golden handshake, if only because their colleagues are watching to see how they will be treated. Poor performance cannot be tolerated, but behind the poor performance lies a human being who must be understood and helped.

Promotion

One way of rewarding a job well done is promotion. Indeed in many fields there is an over-emphasis on promotion, to the extent that many people come to look on their job as just one more rung on the promotion ladder. Much of the working population is still employed in large organizations which have a pyramid structure. Only one man sits at the very top and, by the nature of a pyramid, only a small proportion of people can expect to struggle more than a few rungs up the ladder. Constant emphasis on promotion as a form of reward leads to frustration on the part of those who do not get promotion. It also leads to good technical people accepting promotion into administrative and management posts for which they are not fitted.

So far as possible, every job should be designed to be satisfying in itself. The system of financial reward in the company should be such that a good technical person can be seen to have a route upwards within his technical speciality. In some companies, for instance, a really top-grade technician or professional man can move up a technical non-managerial ladder and perhaps reach the standing of a divisional manager with some such title as principal technical officer. He continues to work at his speciality, where he is of greatest value to the organization. He is probably more content himself to follow his speciality, particularly because the organization has the good sense to give him the status, seniority and salary which he earns.

Any formal salary scale should not just have a single fixed salary for the job. There should also be enough room to allow a man who does the job superlatively well, but is unsuitable for promotion, to be adequately rewarded. The very top rate of pay for a job might, for instance, overlap the starting rate of pay for a job two grades up in the hierarchy.

Rewarding special effort

Large organizations are frequently obsessed with salary scales and frameworks to the extent that it becomes impossible to reward a person for special effort without promoting him or her. Special efforts should be recognized and rewarded. Most people can be persuaded to make an extra special effort once in order to help in achieving some objective. But, if there is no recognition or reward for the effort, it will be a lot harder to enlist their support a second time. The possibility of special one-off bonuses should not be overlooked.

Thanks

This is a small word but it helps a lot. In the last analysis, people of course wish to receive a tangible reward in the shape of increased salary, perks or promotion. They do also, and very much more immediately, wish to be appreciated. They also want other people, particularly their colleagues, to see that they are appreciated. This is an area where a junior manager may play a large part. He may not be able to influence his company's salary policy directly. He can, however, make sure that, where any of his people put up a good performance, it is recognized, and the person gets some praise and public recognition for it. When somebody outside your department does something to help you, a letter of thanks to him or a letter to his manager drawing attention to the good work always helps to give people a feeling of satisfaction and a desire to help next time.

Where your people have performed exceptionally well, they will appreciate a reference to their contribution in published material. If appropriate, a laudatory comment may be placed in the local paper or in a house journal. The divisional manager or some member of higher management may be persuaded on his next visit to stop and talk to the star performers and thank them for their good work. Among professional and technical staff, the opportunity to attend meetings of professional associations in the firm's time is a reward which is sometimes greatly appreciated.

Conclusion

However it is done, your people must be rewarded for their performance against the objectives set them in their current job. Whatever the limitations imposed by the company's personnel and salary policy, the manager must keep this basic principle in the forefront of his mind.

11 On being promoted

The new manager

Sometimes when a manager is first appointed to a job he will be properly inducted into it. He will meet his new senior manager, who will discuss the job with him and say what he expects. The senior manager will introduce him to his predecessor and there will be an adequate handover period. Depending upon the job, this handover period could range from a couple of days to several weeks.

Unfortunately we do not live in a perfect world. It is just as likely that you will simply be told that you have been appointed manager of the blanket section from next Monday morning. The man who appoints you knows what the blanket section is and what it does. There's always been a blanket section in the firm – everyone knows what it is and what it does. The possibility that you don't doesn't enter anyone's head. If you want the job, you have to face the blanket section on Monday morning and manage it. Before you can manage it, you will need to find out where it is, why it exists, what it does and how it does it and, most important, who the people are who form the blanket section. We are concerned in this chapter with coming to grips with the people.

The existing staff

Most people find the unknown frightening. One of the most difficult aspects of taking on a new job as a manager is coming to grips with the existing staff. They know each other, they know the job and the rules, and they will tend to take up a defensive attitude in the face of their new and unknown manager. He is new and unknown even if he has been promoted from within the section or branch. He is new because, whether or not he recognizes it, he is no longer just one of the boys. He, or she, is now the leader to whom the others will turn for direction or guidance. He has to deal with the problems and non-standard situations. It is he who must carry full responsibility for the performance of the section. So, although the emphasis may vary, any new manager taking over a job with existing staff has certain problems to face and certain tasks to achieve. He has to get to know the staff, their capabilities, their shortcomings and their potential; he has to establish in them a feeling of confidence in his ability both to do the job and to look after their interests; he has to persuade them to devote their minds, interest and energy to their job. This is true whether he has been appointed from within the section, transferred in from elsewhere in the company, appointed from another company or appointed directly from school, college or university.

Improvements

When taking over existing staff, it is always wise to take some time to discover the form before you start altering the existing arrangements and method of doing the job. On the first morning, people may come to you with plausible ideas for improving things: 'If only we did so and so how much better it would be.' Be wary. It may be a genuinely sensible suggestion which can bring a marked improvement in the results achieved by the section. It can also be someone trying to settle an old score or trying to land you in trouble. Whichever it may be, give yourself time to consider it. Listen to the suggestion, probe it gently and promise to consider it. Explain that, although it seems a good suggestion to you, you want to find out how the whole section works and fits into the company as a whole before you make any changes. This gives you a breathing space to find out if it really is a good suggestion or just a trap. Don't forget the suggestion or who made it. You must come back to him in the course of the next few days to tell him what you have decided to do about it.

Your notebook

There will be a lot of things you have to remember in the course of your new job. Many of them are things which people tell you and they will be offended if you forget them. If they are not offended, they will realize and resent the fact that your interest in them is superficial. Your interest in your people must neither be superficial nor appear to be superficial. Some people have excellent memories for detail, though most of us don't. In most cases it is helpful to keep a notebook. One of the most important uses of the manager's notebook is for keeping full and confidential notes on his staff. This part of the notebook forms the record of his human inventory.

In large companies, personnel departments keep, as a matter of course, records of every employee, with a personal file containing a copy of every letter from, to or about, the employee since he first applied to join the firm. Some extract or summary sheet containing bare details about the employee is almost certainly provided to some level of line management. It may well not be provided to the lowest levels of line management. Even if it is provided, you still need your own notebook. The mere fact that you compile it laboriously in your own hand helps to imprint the contents in your mind and also allows you to record the facts which you consider important. Secondly, the fact that you carry it in your pocket means that you always have it available when you want it: perhaps at home in the evening or during illness; perhaps on a visit to another part of the company or when with one of its customers or suppliers; perhaps you are at a management meeting and are asked whether you have someone available with a particular aptitude.

The manager's notebook is a key tool and should be constructed as quickly as possible after he is appointed to a job. Thereafter he will keep it up to date as circumstances change. The section dealing with people will be in two parts. First, he needs a summary showing how his human inventory relates to budget. Second, he needs an individual record of every person who works for him.

The individual personal record

It is simplest to consider the individual records first. The layout depends on personal choice and on the size and shape of the notebook which will fit conveniently into the manager's suit pocket or handbag, as the case may be. The heading information is straightforward factual information, which should be available from the company's personnel records or from the previous holder of your job. This information covers: full name, address and telephone number (if any), whether married or single, date of birth, date of joining company, salary, with date and size of last two salary increases, details of any special allowances or expenses payable – for example, for some special qualification or for running a car – formal qualifications – number of 'O' levels or other educational and technical qualifications – title of job.

After these basic items, the remainder becomes a matter of choice and is gradually built up from odd snippets of information picked up over the months. More personal details are useful. For young people, do they live at home? If not, what is the name and address of their parent or guardian? For married people, do they have children? Of what age? Are they at school or university, or at work? Does the husband or wife work and, if so, where? For older people, what is the name and address of their next of kin and do they have any health troubles? For all staff, what are their hobbies and outside interests?

It may seem that all this information is of no concern to the manager. It is personal information and he is just being nosey in trying to secure it. Certainly he should not appear to be prying when it is obtained. Most of it will come to him just by listening. Most people like to talk about themselves. They will talk during breaks, in the canteen over lunch and when they are packing up to go home. On top of that, quite a lot of personal chat will come out in the course of normal working discussions. The information is important to you in your job. It helps you to understand your people. When a married woman becomes a late arriver, looks perpetually worried and is not doing her work properly, it will help you to deal with her in an understanding way and to bring her back on course if you know that she is keen for her only son to have a good education and that he has just taken an important examination a few weeks back.

On the whole, most people do not do poor work from sheer bloody-mindedness. They work badly because they are misplaced in their job, because they are mismanaged or because, for some reason, they are unhappy or unsettled. The unhappiness may be caused by something totally unconnected with work. None the less it affects the quality of the work performed just as surely as an unhappiness arising from the working situation. If you have some idea of the cause of the unhappiness, however vague, it will almost certainly help you in bringing the person back to full productivity.

The facts in these personal records also help you in the

occasional situation where immediate action is needed, as in the case of illness or accident at work. No doubt the personnel officer would sort it all out in due course, but your notebook can help you to take immediate action.

Finally, the personal record should contain information about the training each person has had and comments about their abilities, aptitudes and interests. The fact that someone can type, even though it is not part of their normal job, may be useful on some occasion when typing is urgently needed in order to get a letter into the post after the typists have left the office. An interest in first aid is a more obvious example of the sort of thing that it can be useful to know about. An employee's outside interests can often be used to the benefit of the company on some occasion, if they are known about. The sort of outside interests we have seen put to good account are amateur interests in photography, flower arranging, local history and topography, do-it-yourself, painting, drawing and all sorts of private interests in the electrical, mechanical and radio fields. A man or woman may be an amateur in the sense that their interest is pursued in their spare time, but may none the less be an expert. Not only are their abilities and depth of knowledge frequently as good as full-time workers in the field, but they are usually flattered to be called on from time to time to exercise their skill.

Apart from any possible relevance to the immediate job in hand, the range of outside interests of outwardly quite ordinary people is staggering. Many run their hobbies almost as a part-time business and may make a substantial income from it. Over the years, in the factories and offices in which we have worked we have come across the following: a man who ran a small Christmas tree plantation; a part-time rally driver; breeders of dogs, cats and donkeys; a man who ran a village store; another who operated a part-time insurance agency; a man who translated foreign technical documents from French and another who translated from Russian; people who glide, sail, and pilot fixed wing aircraft; embryo poets and novelists; people who take part in local government, belong to local societies, sit on school and hospital boards and take part in other forms of voluntary work. These interests, we emphasize, are followed by quite ordinary men and women, working for their living in ordinary occupations.

Don't run a gossip shop

In following their hobbies or interests, people may want some special consideration at work. It may help them to leave half an hour early on the first Tuesday in each month, for instance, to go to a committee meeting. If there is a good reason behind it, be sympathetic to such a request, providing the work is still done effectively and on time. It helps to make the people concerned contented in their work and ties them more firmly to the company. Their outside interest may have no direct relevance to their job, but it broadens their outlook. You cannot begin to understand people unless you know about their interests. Most people like to talk about their hobby. The fact that they can talk to you about it helps to create a bond of understanding between you. However, this comes not in a day or two but over a period of months or years. One word of warning: you are not running a gossip shop. Watch that these discussions are kept to the appropriate times and not allowed to last too long. As we said when we were discussing the use of your own time, aimless gossip can run away with a disproportionate amount of your day. None the less management is people and people take time. Some part of this time is legitimately spent in getting to know about them by listening to them. You should also keep a note of their weaknesses. The fact that you keep your notebook in your own handwriting in your own pocket means that it is one of the very few documents which really is confidential and for your eyes alone. Everybody has some weaknesses and it will save a lot of regrets if you recognize from the start that your people, like everyone else, are not perfect.

A major reason for recognizing weaknesses and strengths in your staff is so that this knowledge can be applied in improving the work of your section. One person may be quite incapable of adding up a row of figures and getting the right answer. In days gone by, some members of the BF and BI management would deliberately have given such a man as much work involving addition of figures as possible. This would be done to let him know who was master or 'for the good of his soul'. The consequence would be that the person was miserable, his work output low and the working atmosphere would deteriorate. Modern managers will try to help their staff to overcome their weaknesses, but will concentrate on harnessing each person's strengths to the job, while trying to avoid relying on his performance in the areas of his weakness. There is considerable wisdom in the old Stock Exchange saying that you should cut your losses and run your profits. This applies to people as much as to stocks and shares.

Be objective

As you fill up the individual sheets of your notebook, try to be as objective as possible. Try not to be influenced by your prejudices. You may not like tall girls or men with beards, but these dislikes are totally irrelevant and must not be allowed to influence your judgements. We all have prejudices; it is best to recognize your own and specifically offset them in making your judgements. More seriously, it is essential to avoid discrimination against certain categories of people on grounds of religion, politics, sex, race or age.

As you are getting to know the existing staff of the section, you should be looking out for the informal organization pattern. What are the links between people inside and outside the section which make things happen, and what are the links down which information flows? Which of your staff have lunch together? Who have common interests or club memberships? Who is courting whom? And which beautiful friendships have become unstuck in the past and left sour feelings behind? An understanding of these links may explain many things which happen in the section and which are otherwise inexplicable.

The notebook summary

As well as the individual sheets about each person in your notebook, you will also need a summary. This should list the budgeted staff of the section by grade or job title and show how actual staff present match the budget both in terms of numbers and salary. Depending on the company or the type of work the section is doing, it may be desirable to split budget and actual figures in some other way, such as by sub-section, or class of work, or experience level of the people. The choice depends upon what is meaningful in your particular context. Whatever the choice, it must serve as a reminder of things which need your attention, such as staff recruitment that is needed. Other useful parts of this summary section are: a note of the company salary scales for the types of staff in your section; notes on admissible rates of expenses if this is applicable to your section: notes on holiday entitlements, and a sheet showing holidays for each person in the current year.

Establishing yourself with your people

When you take over a section of existing staff, one of the things you have to do is to establish their confidence in you as a manager. An effective way of starting is to discover what are the minor irritations which impede the section in their work or make life uncomfortable for them. Having done this, try to find a way of overcoming some or all of these problems. For instance, the girls may complain that the towels in the ladies' lavatories are only changed once a week on Monday mornings and are filthy by Tuesday lunch time. Find out who is responsible and chase them to have the towels changed three times a week. Push hard at it. Nobody will want to know, but it is somebody's job to see that there are clean towels. Find out who it is and give them no peace until they perform satisfactorily. Every section has its minor irritations, and a great many of them can be cured if the manager cares enough to find out who is responsible, suggest how an improvement can be made, and keep after the person responsible until it is. One thing every group of people wants in their manager is the ability to get things done. Let your section see as soon as possible that you get things done, even if to start with they are quite minor things. There will be no need to brag about it to them. They will recognize your performance even more certainly than you will recognize theirs.

Dealing with the passengers

When you take over any sizeable section, the chances are that you will find some passengers – people who have just come along for the ride and who are not pulling their weight. Try to discover why they are not pulling their weight and try to persuade them to a better performance. The techniques referred to in the previous chapter will help with this. Among the passengers may well be a hopeless case, an elderly widow who is quite incapable of doing any job properly for instance. Be very patient and careful with such people. They may be alone in the world: they may have some other person completely dependent on them and on their

113

earnings. Your company is not a charitable organization dispensing social security benefits, but it is – if you work for it – humane in its relationships with such people. If they are sacked, they may never get another job. Common humanity demands that you lean over backwards to encourage and help such people to do their work. Remember that everyone has some strong points. Try to find such strong points and if necessary reorganize the work of the section to allow the elderly widow to make her contribution to the section's performance. Although the rest of the section may complain bitterly about her, they are also likely to be all on her side if you sack her. Such action may adversely affect section morale and attitudes, with a consequent fall in the standard of performance.

If your feeling of common humanity does not run very deep, and if you are dedicated to absolute efficiency judged in money terms, pause. Recognize that, in the medium term, your job will probably be done more effectively and more easily if you act considerately in all your dealings with your people. It is not just being soft, for it pays in results. Remember that management is people.

12 Recruiting

A management opportunity

The recruitment of new staff presents an opportunity for every manager. Care and thought in recruitment enable him to improve the performance of his section, cover some of the weaknesses or gaps in the section's abilities and also provide the human basis for the execution of his future plans. When you take over an existing section you have little option but to take the people as you find them and do your best to improve their performance. With new staff, the position is entirely different. You should make every effort to get the best person available for the job in question. Some companies leave recruitment to the personnel department who will provide a clerk, a graduate, a programmer with COBOL experience, a typist, or an HNC electrical engineer on demand. This is not good enough. So far as circumstances allow, you should insist on having a say in the choice of new staff for your section – not only having a say but an opportunity to go over the applicants' papers and to interview a selection of the more promising candidates.

Before any recruitment is started, you will have to define the job and the sort of person you want to fill it. You will also have to obtain approval in principle to recruiting to fill the vacancy. This may be a mere formality if it is a replacement for someone who is leaving, or if budget provision has been made for an extra person in your plans for this year. However, for a totally new job, you will probably have to seek the approval of your own manager. This may initially be given informally in discussion of your current work or future plans. Alternatively, you may have plans to improve the effectiveness of your section. These will have been formalized into a document setting out the nature of your proposals, the benefits which you expect to accrue to the company

115

if the plan is implemented, and a plan for implementation of the proposals. This plan will set out any organizational changes involved, any additional staff required, a timetable and a statement of costs.

Is external recruitment necessary?

Whether such a formal proposal is required or not, considerable thought must be given to the matter before recruitment is initiated. First, what is the job to be done? If Mr Plume, the chief clerk of sub-section A gives in his notice, the easy way out is to say you need a replacement chief clerk for sub-section A. This, on the face of it, is the quickest and easiest way of filling a routine but busy job. It may also be the first reaction of a harassed and over-worked section manager. However, it is passing up an opportunity which should be taken to examine Mr Plume's job and those with which it interacts. Is the job really necessary? This may seem a ridiculous question to ask when Mr Plume gets in early every morning, has his head down all day, and moves a mountain of paper. Now is, however, a good time to ask the question, when there are no overtones of redundancy to cloud the discussion. Careful examination may reveal that, hard though Mr Plume works, his real contribution to the objectives of your section may be slight. Careful scrutiny may show that sub-sections A and B can be united under one chief clerk, while each clerk in the combined sub-section undertakes a little bit more responsibility in his own area.

Maybe it will turn out that Mr Plume's job is essential, in which case you carefully revise the job specification to see that it is up to date. The next step is to consider the sort of person who is required to do it. Once the qualities required have been listed, you are ready to set about filling the job. The first place to look is within your own section; is there anyone fit for promotion to fill the job? If there is, well and good; if not, the next stage is to consider whether anyone can be found inside the company. The problem should be briefly discussed with your own manager, in case he wishes to transfer or promote someone from one of his other sections. Next the personnel officer should be consulted.

Your company may have a plan for rotating staff between different parts of the company, or it may be so rigidly compartmentalized that staff rarely move across the well defined departmental boundaries. Other companies run schemes for the internal advertising of vacancies in the company newspaper or house journal and on the company notice boards. However it is organized, you should try to see if anyone is available internally. By doing this, it may be possible to absorb someone from another department which is being reduced in size. The company does not have to incur the costs of recruitment. These are considerable both in terms of hard cash for advertising and agency costs and interview expenses, and also in terms of indirect costs which are largely your time. Furthermore, someone recruited internally should require less training than a new recruit. He should know a certain amount about the company, its organization and its products. Training of an internal recruit should just be a topping-up process dealing largely with the particular nature of the new job he is to do.

Internal recruiting dangers

There are snags with internal recruiting. Once you have put the process in motion, it may prove difficult to reject someone who you think does not quite fit the bill. You may also be subject to pressure to accept someone who is not right for the job. Some managers are not prepared to face up to sacking people who ought to be sacked, or dealing with people who have been over-promoted. Their way out is to try to arrange internal transfers, thus passing their problem on to some other manager. A variation of this is the manager who passes on his troublemakers. The troublemakers range from those who ought to be sacked – the man who consistently arrives very late in the morning and comes back from lunch drunk every afternoon – to the person who is just a nuisance, for example the malicious gossip. You must do your utmost to avoid being landed with these duds and troublemakers. Don't be content with studying the papers. A poor manager will not only try to pass on his problems, he will also cover up when writing reports on staff. Even an interview may not show up the trouble. In the case of internal transfers, it is always wise to try to glean some information informally by tactful inquiries from your acquaintances in the company; in other words check by means of the grapevine.

Another possible problem with internal recruiting is the 'relative'. If you are offered the company secretary's daughter on transfer from elsewhere in the company, where she is considered suitable, and you turn her down, you are in danger of making an enemy at the centre of the company. Yet if you take her on and she is incompetent, you will be in an even worse predicament. This, like many other problems, is best tackled as soon as it appears. If she seems to you, after careful consideration, to be unsuitable for the job, turn her down as tactfully as possible: perhaps the job will not offer sufficient scope and interest for someone of her ability and intelligence!

Recruitment procedure

If there is no suitable candidate for the job inside the company, external recruitment will be necessary. The routine of this will be handled by your personnel officer. It is probably best to see him or her for a preliminary discussion. Take along a copy of the job description and a profile of the sort of person you are looking for. This profile should give the qualifications and attributes which you are looking for, the salary for the job, the probable age range of the candidate, and an indication of whether you are looking for someone with potential for development. The personnel officer will indicate how he hopes to bring in candidates, from an agency, from personal contact with local schools, technical colleges or universities or from a special or general advertisement in the press. If it is to be by a special advertisement, you should help to draft it. Certainly make sure you see the final draft before it goes to the newspaper.

Whatever the source of external recruitment, the personnel office will in due course pass you a number of letters and/or forms of application for the job, possibly with some comment on their suitability. The applications should be studied carefully. The way in which they have been completed will tell you quite a lot about a person. For someone who has to write reports or write to customers, it should show if he can express himself simply, clearly and concisely. In many more subtle ways, what the applicant chooses to say about himself and the way he says it will give you a clue to the sort of person he is. Even what he has obviously left out is important. Apart from such indications, the application gives you all the facts about the man. The application form and letter are unlikely to tell you which is the right man for the job, but they will tell you who should be rejected out of hand and who should be called in for interview.

Preparing for the job interview

Whether a job is to be filled from internal or external recruitment, applicants will have to be interviewed. Interviewing job applicants is a key management task which is undertaken by all levels of management. Even the chairman or managing director of the largest company has to handle such interviews, if only when filling jobs such as managing directorships of subsidiaries. In their case, the interviews are probably not formal job applicant selection interviews since they will have been carried out discreetly over the months or years as succession planning goes on. Job applicant interviewing, at whatever level, is important. As soon as possible in your first management post you should start to get experience of this vital task. Apart from interviewing to fill your own vacancies, there may be other opportunities. In some expanding companies as part of their general recruitment campaign, they may offer informal interviews to people in a particular town or centre on one or more evenings. The interviews are advertised in the local and national or trade press. They are generally for specialist staff in short supply, such as programmers or certain types of engineer. The interviews are carried out informally to see whether the people who come in might be suitable for the company and, if they might be, to then encourage them to proceed with an application to join. Such interviews are generally carried out by a mixture of personnel staff and line managers. Frequently the personnel department find difficulty in persuading line managers to undertake an extra evening commitment of this kind. They welcome volunteers, and this may prove a good first opportunity to try your hand at interviewing.

Before you start interviewing, you must prepare for it. The circumstances of the interview must be such that the applicant can relax his guard sufficiently for you to learn something of the real person. Your preparations must be aimed at making this possible. Enough time must be allowed for the interview. In most cases a thorough job cannot be done in under three-quarters of an hour, and this time should be free from disturbance from visitors, phone calls or the demands of your secretary or other staff. If you have a secretary, she must be briefed to prevent interruptions. If you haven't, then at the least you should put a 'Do not disturb' notice on the door and tell the switchboard to intercept your phone calls. It is probably preferable to do the interviewing in your own office.

If this is not possible, it should be in some place where privacy is possible. The applicant should not be distracted by what is going on around him, nor should he feel that he can be overheard by staff working nearby. The ideal is clearly a properly closed-off office and not one corner of a large modern open plan area. The interview room/office should be clean, tidy, well lit, adequately heated and ventilated. Even if you do not smoke, have a clean ashtray in the room. If the applicant smokes, it may help to put him at his ease. If your office administration makes it possible, make arrangements for two cups of coffee or tea to be brought in at the beginning of the interview. This also helps to break the ice. Needless to say, you should also have refreshed your memory about the job specification, the profile of the person you are looking for, and the conditions of service – hours of work, amount of holiday, salary, etc. – which can be offered for the job. The letters of application and application forms should be carefully studied and the key points noted; nothing is more irritating to the applicant than an interviewer who, by his questions and conversation, shows he has not read the application form, which has probably been compiled laboriously and with great care.

Some junior managers have been known to carry on an interview with their desk-top littered with papers of all shapes and sizes, while constantly breaking off the interview to take phone calls, and dispensing a succession of instant decisions on trivial matters to a constant stream of interrupters. They believe they are giving an impression of a high-powered troubleshooting executive. They are not; the impression they give is that of an incompetent little man, who is out of his depth.

A seven-point plan

When you are interviewing someone, do not forget that the interview has a purpose: to enable you to assess whether the applicant is suitable for the vacancy you are trying to fill. A secondary purpose is for the applicant to decide whether he wants to accept the job if it is offered to him. How do you set about assessing the applicant? One effective way is to carry on the interview with a view to reaching an assessment of the person on seven key points. Some of these points are more critical than others, but they are all relevant to your decision. The seven points are dealt with in some detail.

1 Superficial impression

Some assessment of a person can be made on the basis of his appearance, bearing and speech. This should not be an opportunity to exercise your personal prejudices about length of hair or style of dress. However, the objective needs of the job should be borne in mind. For instance, at the time of writing, a young man appearing at an interview for a job as a capital goods salesman in the UK, wearing a kaftan, is likely to be unsuitable. Apart from the unsuitability of that form of dress for such a salesman, his appearance would throw doubt on his desire to get the job and also on his judgement.

Quite a lot can be guessed about a man or woman from their appearance. Anyone applying for a job should and probably will be neat, clean and tidy. Some will be dressed in the height of fashion, men as well as girls. Others will be dressed more conventionally. But it is worth noticing if a man has buttons missing from his shirt or jacket, dandruff on his collar or down-at-heel shoes. Are a girl's tights laddered, baggy or crooked, has she loose hairs on her shoulder; if she wears make-up, has it been carefully or sloppily applied? When the applicant comes in, does he appear serene, nervous or over-confident? Does he stand and walk upright or is he round-shouldered and stooping? When he sits down, does he sit relaxed and comfortable, lean on your desk, slouch in the chair or sit nervously on the edge of the chair? Does he talk to you, or to the floor, or to some distant object? Is his speech clear or blurred, pleasant or grating, easy or difficult to understand?

In days gone by, a great many interviews were decided purely on such a superficial assessment. Modern managers do assess applicants under this heading, but it is only one of seven headings and not by any means the most important.

2 Attainments

In most walks of life, we try to predict the future to a large extent from our knowledge of the past and our guesses about how past patterns will be repeated or modified by changing circumstances. So, an important part of our assessment is to look at what the applicant's attainments are. What has he achieved in the past? This must be related to the person's age and opportunities. A school leaver's attainments will be limited to his achievements in school examinations and his sports and hobbies, whereas a man of forty will be expected to have some solid achievements behind him in his working life. Some weight in this assessment must be given to the opportunity for achievement, difficult though this is to judge. For instance, in judging eighteen year olds, we would give greater weight to the one who went to a poor comprehensive school and obtained two 'A' levels, than we would to one who went to a leading public school and obtained several 'A' levels. The first, we assume, has succeeded in the face of considerable difficulty, indicating some persistence and determination. The second undoubtedly has an achievement to his credit, but one which has probably been achieved more easily and certainly in less difficult circumstances. Generally speaking, you want to recruit effective people. It is a hard fact of life that some people are more effective in getting results than others. There are some non-achievers, who always have an excuse for failure. The excuses are full and plausible, but beware of them.

3 Intelligence

Different jobs require different levels of intelligence. No one seems to be too sure what intelligence is anyway. We may be looking for someone with a reasonable amount of nous or common sense. For the majority of clerical, administrative and supervisory posts, this is basically what we are seeking under the heading of intelligence. Some indication can be obtained from the way in which the applicant appreciates and answers your questions. For technical and professional staff, some indication that they have the necessary intelligence for the level of job can be deduced from their qualifications and from the way in which they discuss their speciality and past experience.

4 Aptitudes

In drawing up the profile of the person required to fill the vacancy, you will have listed certain aptitudes as being essential and others as merely desirable. Some aptitudes are difficult to judge at an interview. If, for instance, you are going to take on trainee or junior computer programmers, you will almost certainly want them to be given an aptitude test before you interview them, and will have the results in front of you when you do the interview. An aptitude for self-expression or artistic work may be more easily recognized in the interview itself.

5   Interests

You may aim to find out the applicant's interests. These may range from watching TV, playing the violin, dancing or painting, to rugger playing or social work. You cannot make a valid judgement of a person without having an idea of his interests in life. It is generally an encouraging sign to find that people have a creative interest of some sort or that they play an active rather than a passive role in some field.

6   Disposition

What sort of person is he? Will he get on with the other people in the section? Will he have the right personal characteristics to deal with people outside the section and, if applicable, with customers or suppliers? Is he apparently ambitious? Is he likely to accept responsibility? How suitable does his disposition appear to be for this job?

7   Circumstances

What are his personal circumstances and how are they likely to affect his performance in this job? Is he married or single? Has he children or other dependants? Has he strong ties in the local area: family, schooling, or membership of local clubs and societies? Is he prepared to travel for the company if need be? This divides down into short trips and long trips, travel at home or abroad? Is he prepared to move and settle somewhere?

This may seem a formidable list of enquiries. Not every question will necessarily be relevant for the job which you are trying to fill. However, for almost every job there is something relevant under each of the seven points. Before the interview you should go over the job specification and the personal profile. List under the seven points the things which you think are of importance for this job. Also put down the weighting for this job that you give to each of the seven points. For instance, for a junior secretary a fairly high rating is likely to be given to superficial impression, intelligence, aptitudes and disposition, and a fairly low rating to the other three. For a maintenance man to keep the boilers and heating system going, not a great deal of weight will be attached to superficial impression nor to his interests or circumstances. None the less, they will have some bearing on how he does his job.

The interview

After all this preparation, it is perhaps time to settle down to the interview itself. Don't keep the applicant hanging around when he arrives; if he has to wait because he has arrived far too early, make sure he has somewhere comfortable to wait. Provide something for him to read, preferably something about the company or its products. Collect him yourself from the reception area and take him to the interview room. Relieve him of his overcoat, umbrella, etc. and sit him down. The first task is to put him at ease as quickly as possible. A cup of tea or coffee at the beginning of the interview is a great help, but do make sure it is hot and in a clean unchipped cup. Don't forget that the applicant is summing you and the company up just as much as you are summing him up. In starting the interview, look for something in the application form on which to base a question which will start him off talking to you naturally, preferably something about one of his declared interests. From this you can move into a conversation in which you lead him to tell you the things you need to know. This is the main reason why a good interview takes such a long time. The basic information might be obtainable from a series of questions with yes/no answers, but this gives you very little idea of the applicant beyond that obtainable from his application form and appearance. Try to avoid this type of interview. A free two-way conversation will flow more easily and you will discover things which might otherwise have eluded you. You will also see him more nearly as he will eventually be at work.

As well as obtaining information about the applicant, you have to tell him about the company and the job so that he can judge whether or not he wants to work for you and whether the job is one that he wants. This is probably best done after the applicant has talked to you about himself, his past and his hopes for the future. After you have told him about the company and the job, give him an opportunity to ask questions. You can learn quite a lot about someone from the questions he asks. In this part of the interview, you are in effect selling the company and the job to the applicant. Whether or not you eventually offer him the job, and whether or not he accepts it, you want him to go away believing that your company is a good one. He may talk to other people, both possible future job applicants and the company's customers. The impression you want him to give them is a favourable one. However, don't fall into the trap of overselling either the company or the job.

When describing the conditions of employment, be factual and do not be tempted to promise more than you can in fact offer. Even worse is to give half promises. If the man joins you on the basis of half promises which are not fulfilled, you will in due course have a disgruntled and unhappy man working for you. You are unlikely to go wrong on the main item of salary. Watch that he does not join you under the impression that he will have a private office if, in fact, it will be an office shared with three others. Don't build up a picture of a marvellous canteen, if, in fact, it is a scruffy little room in which pork pies and sandwiches can be bought. Try to keep a sense of perspective in describing the company and its advantages. As well as mentioning any special benefits such as Luncheon Vouchers or free tea in the afternoon break, be careful to mention any rules which could later make difficulties: examples are rules relating to dress, for instance that overalls will be worn or that he will be expected to wear a white collar with a dark suit. There is no need to overstress it, but, if it is a rule, mention it. If staff are expected to work overtime without payment, be certain to mention it. Although such practices are still quite common, there are wide variations in practice. Specific points which you must cover are salary, fringe benefits, if any, the pension scheme, including when the person may join it, whether any removal expenses will be paid on taking up the job, the place of work, the working hours, holidays and a description of the job.

If you decide to make an offer, show him round the place where he will work and introduce him to the people with whom he will work: or, better still, introduce him to one of your people with or for whom he will work. Let that person show him round. This gives the applicant a chance to ask a few more questions rather less formally and enables him to get a feel of the working atmosphere.

Closing the interview

When you are ready to complete the interview, you should

125

consider the next step. If the decision to employ the man lies with you and if you have firmly decided to offer the job, it is probably desirable to say that you or the personnel officer will send him a formal offer of employment in the course of the next few days. If, on the other hand, further interviews will be necessary, for example with your manager, you should try to arrange this interview before the applicant leaves.

Another point to be cleared before he leaves is that he should be offered and paid his travelling expenses for coming to the interview. In most cases they are probably very small and the job applicant may be too nervous to ask for them himself. It is mean not to pay them and creates a very bad impression of the company. Finally, make sure that he gets back his coat and other belongings and is shown off the premises. Afterwards, return the papers to the personnel department with your assessment and decision and check that they actually send a letter turning the applicant down or offering him the job.

13 Redeployment, redundancy and retirement

It is an inescapable part of the modern manager's job that he himself is vulnerable and that part of his own job may be to sack people working for him, when this event has to take place. There is no room for passengers in today's competitive world. The search for ever higher productivity in both public and private sectors means that many people will change their jobs – or just lose them. It is their manager's job to do the firing. Like every other management task, it should be done effectively and humanely.

Redeployment

In the search for higher productivity many people are found to be unsuitable for their jobs. They have to be redeployed either inside or outside the company. Redeployment within the company is handled in the same way as normal internal recruitment. However, more often than not, redeployment is a euphemism for the sack.

Why fire your staff?

The main reasons for firing people who work for you are:

- Misconduct.
- Unacceptable behaviour.
- Incompetence.
- Outdated skills.
- Reorganization and headcount cuts.

The first four of these reasons relate to individuals and individual performance.

MISCONDUCT

The disciplinary code in most large organizations requires instant dismissal for serious misconduct. The law permits this in the United Kingdom and many other countries. None the less we would advise any manager to take advice from his personnel manager before summarily dismissing anyone. It is safer to suspend an employee and send him or her home, while you take advice.

By serious misconduct we mean fraud, theft, abuse of trust, or lack of integrity. Where serious misconduct is admitted or proved beyond doubt then the offender should be fired. It is rarely wise to give a second chance in these circumstances. We say that even though we recognize that the misconduct may arise from problems in the man or woman's home life, or from your own failure to provide adequate supervision or audit procedures. On the other hand, do not make the mistake of treating a minor foolishness as serious misconduct. Wilfully claiming several hundred pounds travel expenses, which have not been incurred, would be serious misconduct. Claiming for some expense at the wrong rate or under the wrong heading almost certainly is not. Similarly, taking a couple of the firm's biros or being unable to account for £5 in the petty cash is hardly serious misconduct.

UNACCEPTABLE BEHAVIOUR

This may seem a strange reason in these permissive days. Yet a man or woman's behaviour can make him or her a liability. Persistent discourtesy to the firm's clients is an obvious example. Alcoholism, although an illness, may also result in unacceptable behaviour. Persistent unpunctuality and behaviour which distracts other employees from their work are also unacceptable. Such behaviour is often unconscious and undeliberate. Counselling by a manager can sometimes help the employee to modify his behaviour. This should certainly be tried before you resort to dismissal. If you sack someone and have to replace them by external recruitment, it can be both expensive and disruptive. It is better to spend some time in trying to obtain the necessary improvement. If in the end you cannot bring about the necessary improvement, you will have to face up to firing the culprit.

INCOMPETENCE

This is a difficult subject to deal with. Why is Mr A incompetent? Has he too little intelligence, education, or training? Is he idle? Does he just not try? Is he in the wrong job? Has he been promoted beyond the level of his competence – a living example of the Peter Principle?

These questions suggest another one. Whose fault is it that Mr A is incompetent? Is it his fault? Is it his manager's fault or the fault of the firm? If a fair share of the fault lies with the manager or the firm, then we have some moral responsibility to seek some solution other than sacking Mr A.

Even if it is Mr A's own fault – in practice unlikely – we have, out of common humanity, some obligation to look for an alternative.

The first thing we need to do is to establish the facts. What is the reason for his incompetence? Could we improve his competence by further training or by improving supervision? Could we restructure the job to eliminate, or at least reduce, the element which causes the difficulties? If it seems that we can solve the problem in any of these ways, we should certainly seek to do so.

Unfortunately, the situation cannot always be remedied. He may just be incompetent – not up to the job. Then, we should look to see whether he could do another job in the firm, even if this means demotion. In the case of a long-serving employee who is likely to buckle down to the new job, the less senior or less responsible job can be made more acceptable by allowing Mr A to retain his current salary and then allowing inflation to erode it gradually to the level at which the new job is rated. He may also be given an appropriately face-saving title to help conceal the loss of status.

Make it as easy as possible for Mr A to accept the job but don't overdo it. If you do, he may not be happy in the job and may feel that he has had his arm twisted. Better in these circumstances to let him go and start afresh with some other firm. If you don't, you may merely be establishing a centre of dissatisfaction. If Mr A has to go, recognize the impact this may have on other staff. Even younger staff may react adversely to what appears to be the harsh treatment of a long-serving member of staff. 'What sort of firm is this to work for?', 'Look what they've done to old A after he's worked for them for over twenty years.' This can be the reaction even when the man is not very popular among his colleagues. However, it does not pay

129

to devise a 'non-job' for someone who is not competent to do his existing job. It is better to make a clean break. In the case of an older man or woman it may be best to arrange early retirement. Many firms are prepared to make such arrangements but prefer not to publicize them.

OUTDATED SKILLS

The fourth reason we gave for firing is when someone has allowed their skills to become outdated. He has failed to adapt to change. He has not kept up to date with developments in his field. In short, he has become obsolete. It would be cynical to suggest that he had reached the point where he might transfer to a post in the training department.

Obsolescence is usually associated with age. As a person becomes older he is often less inclined to change or adapt. He won't bother to learn new ways or understand new ideas; he may just be counting the years till he can draw his pension. He may have convinced himself that the old ways will see him through to his retirement. This may be understandable in people of fifty or sixty. Regrettably, we sometimes see these symptoms in those who are much younger.

At one time you could leave school at fourteen with sufficient education to last a lifetime. Similarly a degree or professional qualification was a meal ticket for life. This is no longer so. The person who does not keep up with developments can become as obsolete as a horsedrawn cab in the streets of London.

You may realize the extent of an employee's obsolescence when you carry out his annual review. It may come to your attention more dramatically because, through ignorance, he has done something which will have costly consequences.

Faced with the problem of obsolescence in one of your people, consider whether a reclamation programme is possible. You do have some responsibility for seeing that your staff keep up to date. A severe jolt, plus the provision of suitable training, may save the obsolete employee and bring him up to the standard necessary for continued employment. Unfortunately, some people are unwilling or unable to adapt to change. If you cannot bring about the necessary reclamation, you must face up to sacking him.

Redundancy

The final reason we gave for firing – redundancy – differs from the other reasons because it is not directly a result of the shortcomings of the individual. Nor is much of the policy to be implemented directly influenced by junior and middle managers. None the less the matter is important to them, if only because they may be on the receiving end.

The need for a redundancy programme may arise for many reasons. Market forces or financial constraints may force retrenchment on a firm. Technological advances may mean that less staff are needed to do the same amount of work. It is not unknown for firms in the information technology industry to require a 20 per cent a year increase in turnover to maintain the same level of employment. In other industries change may occur less regularly but more dramatically with draconian reduction programmes. Redundancy programmes may be required to eliminate overlaps and duplication after mergers and acquisitions.

A firm may move part of its headquarters out of an expensive city centre location, or delegate many previously headquarter functions to its divisions or subsidiaries. It may decide to move its overseas marketing operations away from the home country and to employ nationals based in the overseas territories.

Such structural or policy changes may require the relocation or redundancy of staff. Many people will not move. They select themselves for redundancy by their refusal to move. Ties of family, schools, recreation, friends, and local involvement keep them where they are, even if it means redundancy and even if they do not have another job to go to. Where an office or establishment is being moved, this voluntary redundancy may well provide as much staff reduction as is needed.

Who should go?

Where an establishment has to be closed or a headcount cut has to be implemented, a more difficult problem arises. Maybe some jobs can be found elsewhere in the organization. Who will be offered those jobs? How does a firm select staff for redundancy? At factory floor level, selection will almost certainly be subject to a set of rigid rules agreed with the trade unions concerned. A formula such as 'first in, last out' may well be adopted. This is not appropriate when dealing with managers and professional staff. Here, the prime concern must be to strengthen the firm as a result of the redundancy programme, not weaken it. Selection for redundancy must be done with this in mind. The man or woman who has got by in good times, but who is not really satisfactory in terms of behaviour or effectiveness, or being up to date, will be the first to be selected. When strict criteria are applied it is surprising how many passengers are revealed. The people who are retained must be the people who make a real contribution. Particular problems may arise with staff who deal with the firm's customers.

Consider Mr A. He has a lot of valuable contacts and is thought to be very influential with several of the firm's largest customers. Mr A may not be very good at his job but those links may be very strong and effective. They may be strong enough for Mr A to take the customers with him to his new firm. They may even be strong enough to provide Mr A with a base on which to establish his own competing firm.

On the other hand, Mr A may have been trading on his connections for years. He may be a pleasant fellow with whom customers are happy enough to have an expense account lunch every few weeks. They may enjoy a round of golf with him. Their wives may even enjoy the cocktail and dinner party circuit together. However, this may all be on-the-surface good fellowship. In reality, Mr A's influence may be only marginal. The business decisions may be made on more businesslike criteria. In these circumstances Mr A may safely be made redundant. But what if...? In real life it is often difficult to decide in advance whether Mr A's influence is fundamental or merely marginal.

Another factor to consider is how the selection for redundancy will affect the people who remain in the firm. Despite the natural tendency for people to be concerned primarily about their own fate, they are also concerned about fair play. If they believe the redundancy programme is being used to settle old scores, there will be trouble. It may also be difficult to select all the long-serving 'past it' people. Staff do expect loyalty to be two-way and are likely to react adversely if they feel that older staff have been treated unfairly. However, if reasonably generous conditions can be offered, many older people may be glad to accept early retirement.

An effective way of selecting people for redundancy, after clearing out those who are definitely below par, is to let people select themselves. Many organizations, in both the public and the private sector, pride themselves on securing all their necessary staff reductions by means of voluntary redundancy. Voluntary redundancy schemes have the advantage that managers do not have to make invidious decisions. The people who feel unsettled will leave. Those who stay presumably feel committed to the firm and intend to stay for some time. There is, of course, the danger that all the able and brightest people will leave, while the deadwood hangs on. Top management should also have made certain that the brightest and the best can see a worth-while and rewarding future ahead of them.

The firing interview

After all the agonizing over what to do and who should go, we finally have to face the necessity to sack a man or woman – maybe someone we have known and liked for a long time. This is likely to be a difficult and painful business whatever the reason for the sacking or redundancy. Clearly, the personnel department should be consulted well in advance and it will be one of their responsibilities to advise on the legal aspects of the problem facing the manager.

The prime rule is 'Do as you would be done by'. Being fired is a nasty business. No one likes being sacked. Even if there is generous compensation you feel rejected. You may have given years of service to a firm and now they no longer want you. Feelings of rejection are mixed with anger and hostility.

Always sack people face to face. Line managers should do the job themselves. They should not delegate the firing interview to a personnel manager. It is often desirable for the 'one up' manager – that is the manager to whom the employee's manager reports – to conduct the interview. Sacking people is a line management function. The unpleasant task of selecting people for redundancy or the sack is the line manager's job and he should not shirk from the duty of telling the employee in person.

Firing interviews need even greater care than hiring ones. Allow plenty of time for the interview and ensure that there are no interruptions – nothing less than fire or flood should interfere! Reactions to being sacked vary. Grown men have been known to

133

break down completely. Others have been known to become violent. Most people need time to absorb the news and to regain their composure. The manager must obviously break the news as tactfully and as carefully as possible. However, it doesn't help the sacked person to gloss over the reasons for the sacking if these reasons have been within his or her own control. The interviewing manager needs to plan what he has to say carefully in advance, and should discuss this with the person's immediate manager and the personnel manager.

However inevitable it is that an employee has to be sacked, it usually comes as a shock to him or her. Some people want to argue their case. Others just want to discuss the matter. Some want to ramble on and unburden themselves of long-standing minor grievances. A few may be abusive or even resort to violence. The manager must appreciate that, difficult though the situation may be for him, it is much worse for the person on the receiving end. The manager must be tolerant and realize that things may be said in the heat of the moment which are best forgotten. Let the fired person have his say once you have told him the news. Be patient and listen. Avoid getting into an argument. If he is rude, forget it. He is under great strain and hit by thoughts about a whole new range of problems. This can easily lead to temporary loss of control. You will achieve nothing by arguing or allowing yourself to be provoked into retaliatory rudeness. At best, you will be ashamed of yourself when you cool down. At worst, you provide ammunition to be used against you.

When you sack a man, you have to give him quite a lot of detailed information. When is he to leave? For how long will he be paid? What about holidays that may be due? Does he have share options, a company car or company membership of a health care fund such as PPP or BUPA? How will his pension be payable; or is it transferable to a future employer? The law has quite a lot to say on these points. It is best to hand over a letter covering the main points in the course of the interview. The sacked person may be too disturbed to appreciate and remember many of the detailed points. It will help him – and you – if he can refresh his memory quietly at home afterwards. This is particularly important in relation to financial information, as he may well have to quickly rethink his financial plans and arrangements. He will need to discuss the implications with his family. He cannot do this effectively if he has only a vague memory of what was said.

When you are faced with having to conduct a firing interview, consider the timing carefully. There may well be pressures to hold it as soon as possible after the decision is made, but this should be resisted. Think of the impact on the employee and of the effect on his or her colleagues. Don't sack someone just before Christmas unless delay is impossible. If you fire someone on the day before he sets out on his annual holiday, you wreck that holiday for him. Surely your firm can afford to wait for a few weeks? When it comes to the choice of day it is probably best to fire people on a Friday afternoon so that they can go straight home after the interview and have the weekend to recover their composure and lay their initial plans for coping with the situation.

How long should people remain at work after they have been made redundant or sacked? For serious misconduct, instant dismissal is probably justified and they should leave on the day they are fired. In other cases people should be allowed a reasonable period to round off their work, hand over to their colleagues, and make their own farewells. It is often easier for a sacked man to find a new job while he is still employed rather than when he is unemployed. Being able to job-hunt from the office with the use of a phone and possibly a secretary is a great help. Even a junior employee can be given help with producing his *cv* and advice on job-hunting. Some people will do good work while working out their notice, but the presence of a disgruntled colleague may be an unsettling influence on other staff.

How not to do it

You might think that managers would be considerate and helpful when firing staff, particularly when they have been valuable members of the team for many years. Yet industry abounds with stories of the mishandling of sackings and redundancies. The stories pass into folklore and do the firms concerned untold damage. Here are two from our collection with no names and no comment.

EXAMPLE 1
Following a merger, a small research and development centre was closed. A junior personnel officer came down from headquarters to break the news. No line manager appeared. Some of the projects were to be moved to another centre and others were to be wound

up. One Monday morning a few days later and three weeks before the staff were due to leave, they arrived at work to find the place stripped of furniture and a coach waiting to take them to another company site some thirty miles away.

EXAMPLE 2
Mr A, a director of a subsidiary company of a large electronics firm, drove through the gate one morning. He was signalled to a halt by the security guard, who asked him to park his car and come with him to the managing director's office. The managing director took two minutes to fire him. The security guard escorted him to his office and watched him while he emptied his personal belongings from his desk. The guard collected Mr A's company car and escorted him to the gate.

Retirement

Retirement is one of the major changes which affect the lives of every working man or woman. In our twenties and thirties we probably ignore it and may even despise those who think and plan for it. However the manager must recognize that staff in their fifties and sixties will be influenced in their approach to work by the prospect of retirement.

Some may seek to maximize their pensions and this is a positive motivational factor. Others may merely seek to put in time with the minimum amount of effort. It may well be better to retire these people prematurely and to offer them generous terms to go early. Their influence on other staff could be detrimental to the total effort. The cost of employing such staff is high in terms of national insurance, office space, and other costs over and above actual salary. Similarly early retirement can provide an acceptable alternative to redundancy for those who are in their late fifties.

For those staff who have been with you for a long time and who have reached their final year still firing on all four cylinders, you should consider providing them with help in their retirement planning. This may avoid what could be a traumatic experience for them, and a good employee is worth consideration in this respect.

Conclusion

Throughout this chapter the perceptive manager may have asked himself 'Will I really find myself in any of these situations? Do they not all arise in some way from a management fault in myself or one of my predecessors?' Some probably do, and this merely emphasizes the need to take great care in the selection and ongoing management of your people. Unfortunately none of us is perfect and in any case some circumstances are outside our control. Sooner or later we are likely to be faced with the need to sack someone.

Who was it that wrote of man's inhumanity to man? Remember the basic rule: If you do have to sack one of your people, do it as helpfully and as tactfully as you would like to have it done to you.

PART 4

Managing money

14 Accountancy in management

Accountancy

Most managers will get involved in accounting, whether through budgeting, project management, marketing, sub-contracting, sales management or other tasks.

All managers must be aware that, up to the level of their particular responsibility, they are the master and the accountancy service is a tool. Not a tool to be ignored, however, but one to be treated respectfully in view of the great value of the information it provides. A fitter could assemble an engine without a spanner, but it would not last very long.

There are different interface problems with each management level. A very junior manager in some companies could be forgiven for thinking he was working for 'the accountants' on occasions – answering requests for information on this or that financial achievement to go into the accountants' financial 'porridge'. There does not seem to be any output, merely input, to the 'porridge'. Such experiences are becoming less common and, with the increasing pace of IT and more communication in all fields throughout companies, they should disappear. The junior manager could begin by not only giving information as requested but also asking questions in return and, most important, establishing a friendly and enlightened relationship with the accountant or accountancy assistant. In this way the manager can begin to learn the problems the accountants are trying to solve and where his efforts fit in. With IT direct information paths are becoming more open to the accountants, and the information on results can flow downwards to more people as befits their 'need to know' position.

As you go up the 'tree' of management you will find yourself more involved with finance. Your relationship with the accountants will be that of asking relevant questions in order to manage effectively.

There are three main accountancy bodies:

The Institute of Chartered Accountants   Its members would claim it to be the premier institute of the three as they are involved in most accountancy work. These include year-end accounting; company formations, liquidations and mergers; auditing and taxation, both in private practice and in businesses. In private practice, the Institute is well represented in practically every town.

The Association of Certified Accountants   Its function is similar to that of the Institute of Chartered Accountants and it also has many members in private practice. They probably claim to be nearer to the everyday business situation of entrepreneurs than other accountants.

The Institute of Cost and Management Accountants   The members of this institute are to be found in increasing numbers as more businesses discover that Cost and Management accountants can help them make better use of their limited resources. Their main task is to provide financial management information within the company. As one wag remarked, 'If you want to know how much money you might have made in the year, then the Chartered Accountant will tell you; if you want to make money in the year, ask the Management Accountant to help you'. He was probably a member of the latter institute!

As a manager you could deal with any of the types of accountant listed above. They all involve themselves in providing financial information for management, but taxation, auditing and company formation are usually the special province of the Chartered Accountant. In manufacturing you would be likely to meet a member of the Cost and Management Institute in producing cost and variance information as well as profit and loss accounts.

If you are the owner of a small business you will already have had considerable contact with the Chartered Accountant, in connection with your annual accounts. If your business is big enough you will have a management accountant to look after the everyday financial management information side. Whatever the size of the business, the function of financial and management accounting should be carried out in some way. The annual audit and 'accounting' is not the place to find out critical facts about your business. They should have been discovered much earlier.

In the following chapter we shall be looking at the essential ratios and guidelines that a successful business is likely to employ. It is possible to be successful by ignoring all these rules, but the instances are few. It is therefore essential for managers who hope and plan for promotion to have an understanding of accountancy and its relevance in assisting the success of the company. The basics of accountancy is outside the scope of this book, but we shall concentrate on important issues and measurements that define the success or otherwise of a business operation.

Definition of financial management

There are bound to be different explanations as to the substance of financial management, but in essence it is the conversion into monetary terms of the essential actions of management. These are:

- Planning future actions.
- Organizing the company to carry out the plans.
- Controlling the company to allow this to happen.
- Monitoring the actions.
- Re-planning where necessary.

The Institute of Cost and Management Accountants in its 'Terminology of Management and Financial Accounting' defines management accounting as 'the application of professional knowledge and skill in the preparation and presentation of accounting information in such a way as to assist management in the formulation of policies and in the planning and control of the operations of the undertaking'. This concise explanation matches the essential actions of management.

It is clear that no business can work without finance: what we have to do is to define more clearly the relationship between the 'types' of money.

A company is to be set up to make and sell a new product in the retail trade. The total planning will stem from careful marketing information on the likely volume and timing of sales. There will be a demand for **capital**. The calculation of the amount will be based on detailed planning of the costs of:

- A factory.
- Plant and equipment.
- Staffing.
- Product distribution.
- Marketing.
- Financing of debtors.
- Cost of finance and other costs.

The costs will be offset, in due course, by:

- Money from sales.
- Goods obtainable within certain credit time limits which will offset costs for that time.

Some of the initial capital will not be available to spend on a day-to-day basis. This is the **fixed assets**:

- Purchase of factory.
- Purchase of plant, vehicles and equipment.

In the case outlined above there will be plenty of work for skilled accountants. Out of all the planning must come four highly important sets of financial information:

- Cash flow profile.
- Working capital needs.
- Fixed assets financing.
- Profitability.

Accurate planning of these, and continuous knowledge of their state, are vital if a business is to succeed.

Working capital

It is not possible to put these four components of a business operation into an order of merit, but we commence with **working capital** because it immediately allows us to include other useful items. Figure 5 shows how working capital is formulated – basically from **current assets** less **current liabilities**, but, in the process, the diagram shows the make-up of the various parts of those assets and liabilities. There will be extra components in larger company accounts layouts but the fundamentals do not change. Working capital, or more properly the lack of it, is a significant reason for failure in business. The commonest cause of lack of working capital is probably **overtrading**. This is expansion

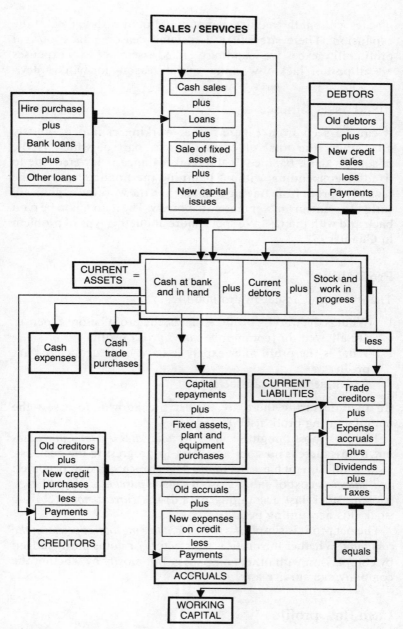

Figure 5 The formulation of working capital

145

of sales without the requisite amount of liquid cash to pay for the expansion. There are other associated reasons: lack of real profitability, excessive spending on fixed assets, or heavy expenses are all part of 'lack of working capital' reasons for bankruptcy.

Fixed asset finance

It can be seen from Figure 5 that working capital is directly affected by the total of current assets, part of which is the business's bank balance. If the bank balance is lowered due to fixed asset spending, without planning the finance for it or the reward in profit from having spent it, then the working capital will suffer. It is not an answer merely to borrow. The loan has to be paid back and with interest. We speak more about this type of problem in Chapter 17.

Profitability

There are three issues in profitability:

1   What is the trading profit? – that is, the profit before expenses are allowed for (commonly called **gross profit**)
2   What is the profit after expenses have been deducted? (**net profit**)
3   Are these profits satisfactory?

(In manufacturing there are further breakdowns to assess the manufacturing profit itself.)

The gross profit might seem to be: *total sales less total purchases* but, unless there is no stock and work-in-progress in the business, a stock adjustment has to be made. The gross profit now becomes: *total sales less* **cost of sales**. Cost of sales is *purchases plus old stock* (closing stock last accounting period) *less current stock* (closing stock this accounting period).

The net profit is simply *the gross profit less the total expenses of the company*. Whether the profit is satisfactory or not is partly judged by comparison with other companies, but mostly by whether the company can survive and prosper.

Cash flow profile

Figure 6 shows the cash flows that might occur in a factory which

REF.	CASH FLOW FORECAST (Months 1 to 12) £000s	1	2	3	4	5	6	7	8	9	10	11	12
	RECEIPTS												
A	Cash sales	—	—	—	5	7	8	10	10	8	10	10	16
B	Debtor payments	—	—	—	11	20	50	90	85	130	120	135	140
C	VAT from C & E	—	—	—	—	—	—	—	—	—	—	—	—
D	Bank loans	300	—	—	—	—	—	—	—	—	—	—	—
E	Sale of assets	—	—	—	—	—	—	—	—	—	—	—	—
F	Other receipts	—	—	—	—	—	—	—	—	—	—	—	—
G		—	—	—	—	—	—	—	—	—	—	—	—
H	Total receipts	300	—	—	16	27	58	100	95	138	130	145	156
	EXPENDITURE												
J	Purchase – cash	—	—	—	2	1	2	3	3	3	3	3	3
K	Purchase – creditor payments	—	—	10	20	25	35	35	32	35	35	35	40
L	Capital expenditure	200	50	10	—	—	5	—	—	—	—	—	—
M	Hire purchase	—	—	—	—	—	—	—	—	—	—	—	—
N	Leasing costs	—	—	—	—	—	—	—	—	—	—	—	—
P	Bank charges and interest	—	—	—	—	—	1	—	—	—	—	—	—
Q	Loan repayments	—	6	6	6	6	6	6	6	6	6	6	6
R	VAT to C & E	—	—	—	—	—	—	—	—	29	—	—	41
S	Taxation	—	—	—	—	—	—	—	—	—	—	—	—
T	Overhead expenses	3	5	5	5	4	4	4	4	4	4	4	4
U	Wages and salaries	25	28	28	35	40	48	48	48	50	50	50	51
V	Other expenditure	—	—	—	—	—	—	—	—	—	—	—	—
W	Total expenditure	228	89	59	68	76	104	96	43	127	98	98	148
H – W	Net cash flow in (out)	72	(89)	(59)	(52)	(49)	(46)	4	2	11	32	47	8
	Opening bank bal. CR or (DR)	150	222	133	74	22	(27)	(73)	(69)	(67)	(56)	(24)	23
	Closing bank bal. CR or (DR)	222	133	74	22	(27)	(73)	(69)	(67)	(56)	(24)	23	31

Figure 6 Cash flow forecast (months 1 to 12)

147

is starting up. The positive cash flow turns to a negative one and then recovers as trading commences. This is a planned process from careful estimates of all the factors involved. Initially, in setting up the factory and distribution network, buying plant vehicles and equipment, purchases, etc., cash will be flowing out of the company and no trading taking place. Capital will be needed to supply this outgoing cash. In fact, the cash flow turns negative. After the business begins to output goods with sufficient profit, the cash flow changes back to a positive one. Many companies have a financial model on their computer so that adjustments to cash flows and other key items can easily be effected. This is an aid, not a substitute, for management decisions on the company operation. In Figure 7 the cash flows have been drawn as a graph which helps to show their movement.

A general cash flow statement is often drawn up in companies to show the overall position, for example:

Cash source	£
Profit before tax	10,000
Add back depreciation provision	3,000
New share issue	5,000
Increase in creditors	5,000
Decrease in debtors	2,000
Total effective cash input	25,000
Cash application	
Dividends paid	(2,000)
Tax paid	(2,500)
Fixed asset purchase	(10,500)
Stock increase	(8,000)
Increase in bank balance	2,000

Conclusion

The four key issues, which stand reiteration, are:

- Working capital.
- Profitability.
- Fixed asset finance.
- Cash flow profile.

To aid in the determination of the correct 'mix' of all the factors stemming from these issues, a number of measurements are

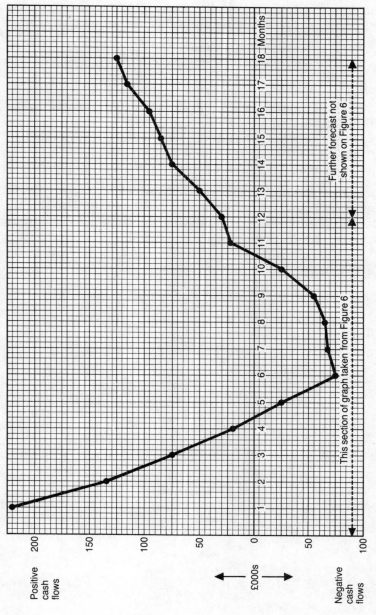

Figure 7 Cash flow forecast

149

currently used. Any company must, however, first survive before it can prosper and grow and the basic rules have not changed despite many changes in the world financial scene:

- Profit is no good if you cannot pay the rent.
- Survival is not easy with a prestigious factory and no money to pay the rates.
- Borrowing money cannot go on for ever (not in normal business anyway). Profit has to be enough to build up the working capital.
- Fixed assets have to earn their keep in one way or another, otherwise they drag the business down.
- Sales are no use if you run out of money (overtrading).

These are a few of the possible pitfalls which a company has to avoid in its search for prosperity and growth. In the next chapter we look into the ways of measuring the vital signs of how a business is prospering.

15 Financial and management accounting

Guidelines

We have seen in Chapter 14 that the total scope of financial and management accounting is larger than we could cover in this chapter. We concentrate therefore on those guidelines and measurements which a company can employ to make itself not only survive but prosper.

There are three guidelines which any normal business must follow to properly serve its shareholders, its employees and the community:

1 A business exists to make a profit. Without profit the business will cease to exist (unless it is subsidized from outside).
2 Unless there is sufficient liquidity in the business (working capital) to pay creditors and other items as they need to be paid, then it will also fail.
3 The profit must be sufficient to provide dividends; to replace fixed assets; to pay for any research and development required; and to repay loans, otherwise there is an increased chance of ultimate failure.

Ratios

To assist in the examination of the state of a business we can employ a series of ratios. Most managers would divide these into three groups as follows:

1 Trading or operating ratios
2 Financial structure ratios
3 Those ratios relating to shares and dividends

We shall treat the last two groups as one, and we also prefer to bring two ratios out of the financial set and treat them separately. We call them the 'Survival' ratios.

A fictional set of accounts for 'The XYZ Wholesale Company', shown in Tables 1 and 2, helps to illustrate the principles. Items are labelled FA1, CA2, etc. for easy reference.

Table 1 *Balance sheet of the XYZ Wholesale Company as at 31 December 19 . .*

Fixed assets				
(after depreciation)				
Freehold premises	(FA1)	169,000		
Plant and machinery	(FA2)	20,000		
Fixtures and fittings	(FA3)	11,000		
Motor vehicles	(FA4)	28,000		
Total fixed assets			(FAT)	228,000
Current assets				
Stock	(CA1)	48,000		
Debtors	(CA2)	29,000		
Cash at bank	(CA3)	27,000		
Cash in hand	(CA4)	1,500		
Total current assets			(CAT)	105,500
Total assets			(TAT)	333,500
Less current liabilities				
Creditors	(CL1)	26,000		
Proposed ordinary dividends	(CL2)	15,000		
Corporation tax	(CL3)	9,000		
Total current liabilities			(CLT)	50,000
Net assets			(NAT)	283,500
Capital				
200,000 of £1 ordinary				
shares fully paid	(OS1)	200,000		
50,000 preference shares 9%	(PS1)	50,000		
Profit and loss account	(PL1)	33,500		
Total capital			(TCT)	283,500

Table 2 *Trading account, Profit and loss account and Appropriation account of the XYZ Wholesale Company as at 31 December 19 . .*

Trading account

Opening stock	(OST)	40,000	Sales (SA1)		285,000
Purchases	(PC1)	199,000			
		239,000			
Less closing stock	(CST)	48,000			
		191,000			
Gross profit	(GP1)	94,000			
		285,000			285,000

Profit and loss account

			Gross profit b/d (GP1)	94,000
Administration expenses	(AX1)	10,000		
Sales expenses	(SX1)	20,000		
Distribution expenses	(DX1)	10,000		
Finance expenses	(FX1)	10,000		
Depreciation	(DP1)	18,000		
Net trading profit	(NP1)	26,000		
		94,000		94,000

Appropriation account

Proposed ordinary share dividend	(OSD)	15,000	Balance of unappropriated profits from previous years	36,000
Preference dividend paid	(PF1)	4,500		
Corporation tax	(CTX)	9,000		
Balance of profits	(APT)	33,500	Net profit this year (NP1)	26,000
		62,000		62,000

Survival

This invariably means just managing to pay bills, more or less on time, but with no apparent prospect of gaining the initiative in terms of profits and further growth. This is not a desirable state for any business but it may be better than bankruptcy if there are hopes of recovery. Some small businesses exist in this state because some sort of living is being obtained for the owner, but they have little to guard them against even a small recession in their business. If fixed assets have to be replaced, borrowing will be resorted to, which will reduce liquidity still further unless there is an improvement in profitability and working capital.

The measure of liquidity is called the **acid test** or **quick ratio** and is expressed as:

$$\text{Quick ratio} = \frac{\text{Current assets (not including stock)}}{\text{Current liabilities (excluding long-term loans)}}$$

The ratio should not be lower than 1, since it is assumed that if it is 1 then creditors could be paid as debtors pay. Although the test is a stringent one, there are other factors involved. If the age of some creditor accounts is up to the limit and debtors are well paid up, one creditor could press hard and an uncomfortable, if not drastic, situation could result. Since there may be cash outputs such as wages etc., even the ratio of 1 may not be enough.

Conversely, some businesses can run with a much lower ratio in cases where large cash sales exist, and money is coming in before bills need to be paid. An example would be a food market. If the ratio is not only low but getting lower, then cash flow problems may not be far behind. The XYZ Company ratio is:

$$\text{Quick ratio} = \frac{\text{Current assets (less stock)}}{\text{Current liabilities}} = \frac{CAT - CA1}{CLT} = \frac{105,500 - 48,000}{50,000} = 1.14$$

This is acceptable, as it is over the preferred minimum of 1 for this ratio, and cash at the bank is nearly 50 per cent of the current assets.

Beyond survival and the 'acid test', is the same ratio but including stock in the current assets. This is called the **current ratio**.

$$\text{Current ratio} = \frac{\text{Current assets}}{\text{Current liabilities}} = \frac{CAT}{CLT} = \frac{105,500}{50,000} = 2.1$$

The textbook value for this is not less than 2; the example shows 2.1, which is satisfactory. However many well known companies operate with figures well below this. In any one company it will vary year to year, but from our own experience in company operation we prefer it not to fall below 1.5. A low figure can be risky; some falling away in the amount of business, or some unexpected occurrence, and the business could be in trouble.

Loan repayments may be distinctly inconvenient, especially if no re-financing can be done. A higher-than-normal current ratio may not be cause for celebration. Stocks or cash could be unduly high and thus investment is inefficient. Stocks could be high but practically worthless (out of date, wrong type, spoiled, etc.). The only real way of ensuring that the ratio is right for a particular business is the time matching of inputs and outputs as detailed on a cash flow chart.

Trading or operating ratios

It is possible to play with ratios and miss some other vital sign, so we cannot assume that ratios are the final answer. One firm may happily prosper and yet certain ratios may not be as good as those in another company. There could be an explanation for this in the use of assets or in the historical placing of the business in a certain part of the country. The comparison with another company may not be sufficiently accurate. The Centre for Inter-Firm Comparison Limited can assist with ratio comparisons where they are possible. Comparisons which are wide of the mark are ineffective and could be useless or even harmful if wrong actions ensue. The main point about ratios is their value in a particular company where they can be compared over a period of years using the same rules of composition.

In general all companies would like to maximize sales and profit while keeping the capital employed as low as possible. The grouping of these ratios is shown in Figure 8.

There is considerable variance between companies on the likely outcome of such ratios: a business producing computer software may have relatively little capital investment compared to, say, a

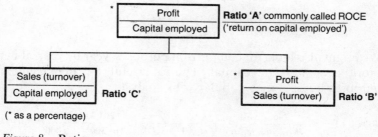

Figure 8 Ratios

155

large engineering company. The software business would not find ratio 'A' as interesting as ratio 'B', where a large profit over sales figure would be their goal. In the case of the company having a large capital base, the profit over capital ratio 'A' would be important. Both the 'profit' and the 'capital employed' are subject to different interpretations by analysts, dependent on the viewpoint to be stressed.

ROCE (RETURN ON CAPITAL EMPLOYED)
It will be seen that ratio 'B' multiplied by ratio 'C' will equal ROCE (ratio 'A'), hence the association of these three ratios.

ROCE is used in different ways by different analysts and managements and, while immediate judgement is useful – for example, an investment comparison – the comparison over several years is a strong feature. If the 'capital employed' is total capital, ROCE can be affected by valuation of fixed assets and possible changes to depreciation (for example, value up; depreciation up; ROCE down). In our example, ROCE (1) gives an overall view, with total capital (normal balance sheet computation) and profit before tax and preference dividends.

$$\text{ROCE (1)} = \frac{\text{Net profit}}{\text{Total capital}} = \frac{\text{NP1}}{\text{TCT}} = \frac{26,000 \times 100}{283,500} = 9.17\%$$

This is not a particularly good result, but many businesses do carry on because of overall advantages, including cars, salaries, pensions, dividends, etc., where the directors own the shares. They also own the general risks of business!

From the viewpoint of the ordinary shareholder, the return on equity capital, using net profit less tax and preference dividends, might be better.

$$\text{ROCE (2)} = \frac{\text{Net profit}}{\text{Equity capital}} = \frac{\text{NP1} - \text{CTX} - \text{PF1}}{\text{OS1} + \text{PL1}}$$

$$= \frac{(26,900 - 9,000 - 4,500) \times 100}{(200,000 + 33,500)} = 5.3\%$$

We might also look, for comparison purposes, year by year, at net profit over working capital. This is useful for management purposes but is not so popular with analysts.

$$\text{ROCE (3)} = \frac{\text{Net profit}}{\text{Working capital}} = \frac{\text{NP1}}{\text{CAT} - \text{CLT}} = \frac{26,000 \times 100}{105,500 - 50,000} = 46.85\%$$

156

It is very difficult to comment sensibly on this figure, as businesses vary greatly. If the percentage is low, it is likely that profits are too low to sustain any growth, but if the business has little in the way of fixed assets a lower figure may be acceptable.

THE OTHER RATIOS

The ratios 'B' and 'C' should use, for comparison purposes, the same profit and capital figures as used in the ROCE calculations. Using NP1 and SA1:

$$\text{Ratio 'B'} = \frac{\text{Profit} \times 100}{\text{Sales}} = \frac{\text{NP1} \times 100}{\text{SA1}} = \frac{26,000 \times 100}{285,000} = 9.12\%$$

This profit is after expenses have been deducted from the gross profit and therefore we can see the effects of the expenses. If the ratio is not up to standard, but the gross profit is acceptable, then an examination needs to be made into:

- Each group of expenditure to see if savings can be made.
- Increasing the sales without depletion of working capital (overtrading) or raising the expenses pro rata.

The profit over sales ratio is one of the commonly used ratios and can vary greatly. A supermarket chain having a high volume of sales at low margins might only have a 3 to 4 per cent profit while an information processing business might enjoy 30 per cent. Once again, the real value of the figure is its suitability for the business concerned and how it compares with others in the same industry.

In ratio 'C', sales divided by capital employed, we get a measure of efficiency in the use of capital but it is not highly reliable. A typical problem is the case of a rising ratio because of sales growth, but production plant and equipment not being kept up to date. Under such circumstances the ratio would be misleading to say the least.

$$\text{Ratio 'C'} = \frac{\text{Sales}}{\text{Capital}} = \frac{\text{SA1}}{\text{TCT}} = \frac{285,000}{283,500} \simeq 1.0$$

We have seen that profit over sales or profit over capital are two measures of profitability, but others have emerged more strongly in the last two decades.

PROFIT PER EMPLOYEE

It has been the practice over many years for the 'workers' to be subjected to many exercises in 'time and motion', 'piece working', productivity schemes, group bonuses, etc. There has been an increasing extension of this to *all* people who work in a company. Not only should we measure the profit over sales and the profit over net assets as before, but we should include a 'profit per employee' figure (which can be split down, if desired, to show parts of a company). This is a valuable measurement and can be compared fairly easily with appropriate competitors. In addition, a 'turnover per employee' figure can be assessed.

PROFIT/SALES RATIOS

We can extend the previous look at profit by splitting it into two parts, each ratio being valuable as a means of searching for further profitability.

Ratio 'D'	Ratio 'B'
$\dfrac{\text{Gross profit}}{\text{Sales}}$	$\dfrac{\text{Profit}}{\text{Sales}}$

The ratio 'D', gross profit over sales, is an important start to profit hunting. If it is too low, net profits may be very difficult to obtain because of overhead expenses. The gross profit percentage would call into question whether:

● Trade goods and/or services are too expensive.
● There are better buying discounts to be negotiated.
● Any in-house manufacturing costs are too high.
● Selling prices could be raised.
● The gross profit is typical (not easy to find out).

$$\text{Ratio 'D'} = \frac{\text{Gross profit}}{\text{Sales}} = \frac{\text{GP1}}{\text{SA1}} = \frac{94,000 \times 100}{285,000} = 32.98\%$$

32.98% is probably good for a wholesale company which has to work on many lower margins than this, but low for a jewellery retailer.

There are then three ratios which are used extensively by management to monitor stock turn, debtors and creditors.

STOCK TURN

Ideally we want to turn over the stock as often as possible. The measurement is usually cost of sales over average stock (half the opening stock plus half the closing stock). In the example it is:

$$\frac{SA1 \times (100 - GP1)}{(OST + CST) \times 0.5} = \frac{285,000 \times 0.67\ 02}{(40,000 + 48,000) \times 0.5} = \frac{191,000}{44,000} = 4.34 \text{ times}$$

Again there is no rule on what this figure should be, and some parts of the stock will enjoy a much higher turnover than others. A thorough examination of slow-moving lines relative to their value in the business can often result in eradication and improvement in the stock turn. In a small business the problem is so often the apparent need for multiplicity of stock coupled with a low stock turn.

DEBTOR LAG

Debtor control is vital for all businesses. If the time of collection is allowed to increase, cash flow problems can commence. The collection time may be shown as a ratio of sales or, as we prefer, a collection time in days.

$$\frac{CA2 \times 365}{SA1} = \frac{29,000 \times 365}{285,000} = 37 \text{ days (approx.)}$$

This would be a good figure for a wholesale company to achieve as it tends, unfortunately, to be nearer to fifty or sixty days in many companies.

CREDITOR LAG

This can be treated in the same way as debtors to obtain a payment lag time:

$$\frac{CL1 \times 365}{PC1} = \frac{26,000 \times 365}{199,000} = 48 \text{ days (approx.)}$$

This indicates that invoices are being paid by the end of the month following the date of invoice which would be satisfactory for most suppliers. Some may insist on thirty days or less.

Financial ratios and share/investment ratios

This subject concerns itself with the method of financing the company and here we can only give an outline. The use of money

159

is always subject to the prospects of reward and a company can obtain money in four main ways:

1　Ordinary shareholding funds
2　Preference shares
3　Loan capital
4　Bank overdraft

The comparison of these funds with the capital employed by the company shows aspects of what is termed **gearing** (sometimes leverage). The principal ratio is:

$$\frac{\text{Borrowings}}{\text{Shareholding funds}} = \frac{\text{PS1}}{\text{OS1} + \text{PL1}} = \frac{50,000}{200,000 + 33,500} = 0.21$$

In low-geared companies, most of the capital is shareholding funds as distinct from borrowed funds. In high-geared companies, the shareholders sometimes see all the profits going to fixed interest loan sources in lean times. The result above shows that the company is low-geared.

The other ratio is:

$$\frac{\text{Borrowings}}{\text{Capital employed}} = \frac{\text{PS1}}{\text{TCT}} = \frac{50,000}{283,500} = 0.18$$

Again a low gearing is indicated.

The ideal gearing must vary from company to company. With a car, a high gear should only be used at high speed: if you go up a hill, you have to change to a lower gear, otherwise you may stall. In a company, a similar state exists: high gearing calls for even more longer-term planning in case that 'hill' appears. It takes much longer to change the gearing in a company.

Public companies depend a great deal on their 'share value', as it may dictate the ease or otherwise of obtaining capital, valuation on a takeover, or simply the day-to-day stability of the company. In particular, a low share value can attract a marauding takeover bidder. There are a number of calculations and expressions in common use as follows:

EARNINGS PER SHARE

$$\frac{\text{Net profit less tax less preference and other fixed dividends}}{\text{Number of ordinary shares}}$$

$$= \frac{\text{NP1} - \text{CTX} - \text{PF1}}{200,000} = \frac{26,000 - 9000 - 4500}{200,000} = \frac{12,500}{200,000} = £0.0625 \text{ per share}$$

THE PRICE/EARNINGS RATIO OR P/E RATIO (PER)

This is the market price (of the share) divided by the earnings per share (or how many years it would take the earnings to equal the market price). If the XYZ company was a public company the PER would be (assuming the market price to be 50p per share):

$$\text{PER} = \frac{£0.5}{£0.0625} = 8$$

The first thing to notice is that the PER will be directly dependent on the price of the share, which will vary in the market. A company will therefore be aware that although it may have direct control on its dividends, the PER can vary because of:

- External market conditions; world/local politics or employee stability.
- The market view on the gearing of the company (low gearing more stability).
- The effectiveness of the present management and known plans.

EARNINGS YIELD

$$\frac{\text{Earnings per share} \times 100}{\text{Market price per share}} = \frac{£0.0625 \times 100}{£0.5} = 12.5\%$$

The earnings yield is the inverse of the PER, but expressed as a percentage. The product of the two numbers will always be 100.

DIVIDEND YIELD

This is what the shareholder actually gets, as distinct from what the company earns. The dividend per share is 15,000 divided by 200,000 = £0.075.

$$\text{Dividend yield} = \frac{\text{Dividend per share} \times 100}{\text{Market value of share}} = \frac{£0.075 \times 100}{50p} = 15\%$$

Of further interest is the value per share of the ordinary share capital. In this case we have £200,000, proven by the balance sheet to have assets behind it, plus the profit added from the appropriation account of £33,500 = £233,500. Over 200,000 shares, the value per share is £1.168.

161

We have not covered all the ratios, but, as far as the trading and operating ratios are concerned, all the important ones have been described. In the financial and investment area, most have been covered and the remainder probably belong to more advanced studies and market analysis experts.

Added value

This is a relatively modern concept of showing the application of a defined profit (or **added value**) to defined expenditure. There is not a rigid rule as to layout but the example below from the 'XYZ Wholesale Company' is typical (see Table 3).

The application usually refers to:

- Wages and salaries.
- Dividends.
- Taxation.
- Depreciation.
- Retained profits.

It is a further move for companies to make their accounts more

Table 3   *Added Value Statement of the XYZ Wholesale Company as at December 19 . .*

Sales	285,000	(SA1)
Cost of sales	(191,000)	(OST + PC1 - CST)
Overhead expenses (excluding those detailed below)	(30,000)	(*)
Added value	64,000	
Application of added value		
Ordinary shareholders dividend	15,000	(OSD)
Preference shareholders dividend	4,500	(PF1)
Corporation tax	9,000	(CTX)
Wages and salaries	20,000	(*)
Depreciation	18,000	(DP1)
Retained profit	2,500	
Application total	64,000	

Notes: Items marked * were not previously defined
The Profit and Loss Account balance brought forward from last year has been depleted by £2,500 (APT)

Table 4 *Layout 1*

	Source	Application
Capital: Ordinary shares	200,000	
Preference shares	50,000	
Fixed assets		228,000
Stock		48,000
Debtors		29,000
Cash		1,500
Bank		27,000
Creditors	26,000	
Dividends (Ordinary)	15,000	
Tax	9,000	
Profit carried forward	33,500	
Totals	333,500	333,500

explicit and meaningful to the reader, bearing in mind that certain information is not willingly given to competitors.

Source and application of funds

These show the accounts in a different light: where the money comes from (in total) and where it goes to. See Table 4.
Normally the period changes will be known and another layout can be used (not from XYZ Wholesale). See Table 5.

Table 5 *Layout 2*

	Period start	Period end	Funds	
			Source	Application
Fixed assets	£10,481.00	£10,981.29		£500.29
Stock	£25,318.69	£21,163.53	£4,155.16	
Debtors	£24,536.18	£25,162.21		£626.03
Cash in hand and at bank	£1,123.00	£3,607.90		£2,484.90
Loans out	£1,565.36	£2,484.73		£919.37
Creditors	£23,108.90	£19,997.12		£3,111.78
Hire purchase	£3,646.00	£1,646.06		£1,999.94
Bank loan	£3,332.03	£2,422.03		£910.00
Net profit			£6,397.15	
Totals			£11,298.32	£11,298.32

The rules of the source and application placing are as follows.

- Funds are *applied* if there is an *increase* of assets, cash at bank, debtors, or loans out, or a *decrease* of loans in or cash in.
- Funds are *sources* if there is a *decrease* in assets, cash at bank, debtors, or loans out, or an *increase* of loans in, or creditors.

This assumes normal circumstances, such as sale of stock or assets, although the profit (or loss) will balance the account accordingly.

Conclusion

In the final analysis a business must make enough profit to replace worn out assets, pay for expansion (if relevant), maintain the real value of capital against inflation, and have enough left over to pay a reasonable dividend to the shareholders. Cash flow forecasts are of inestimable value, especially in capital intensive companies, in determining whether or not profit is sufficient to maintain all these needs without a fall in liquidity.

16 Budgeting and performance

Economic performance

All business involves maximizing economic performance. If it does not, it will be unable to carry out the very plans which ensure its continued existence and its obligations to staff, shareholders and others. These simple statements are the foundations for a complex of management actions to achieve the best economic performance. The goods, supplies and services which are the output of the business must be produced to such a quality, timing and price that customers will continue to purchase the output.

Some will argue that the supply of a service should go on virtually irrespective of the cost, and that economic performance is irrelevant. We assume that the business, service or other environment in which you operate has to succeed in its economic performance. All managers must contribute towards this performance, or they are not managers but passengers. It is unlikely in the business world of the foreseeable future that any room for passengers will exist: the demand for excellence will increase and the less able will not be wanted.

How does budgeting start?

A budget is a written set of plans for the next time phase of a business, expressed in financial terms. The budget establishes specific goals for future operations and actual results are monitored against them. The time phase is usually a year for tactical operational budgets, with longer periods for strategic planning. In some industries a ten-year plan may be necessary – for example, oil or mining. The tactical budget may be further sub-divided for checking purposes into half years or quarters. Close monitoring of results and corrective action can then take place.

When a company starts to sort out its next year's budget, it will do so several months ahead. It will study the following information:

1 The target profit growth which it believes is necessary to ensure survival, provide funds to pay for capital equipment, acquisitions, loans and dividends.
2 The market potential for its type of business or acquisition.
3 The likely effects of governmental decisions (here and abroad, if applicable), in terms of taxation and capital allowances, or any political considerations affecting trade generally.
4 The resource position of the business in terms of cash, borrowing ability, people and management capability.
5 Previous budgets, achievements and shortcomings.

It is important in any company that budgets are constructed not only from the views of top management but from lower management as well. No budget should ignore this principle because goals which have to be achieved must be agreed with the achievers, whatever their position in the company. It will be clear from looking at the five main criteria above that they are interlinked. All budgets are a compromise between forces pulling in various directions: the desire for maximum profit; the acceptable degree of risk; the ability to get and utilize effectively the resources, either money, material or human; and the constraints of the market-place. It should be equally clear that no part of the organization should escape from looking at its particular part in the overall jigsaw of the budget. Figure 9 shows the components and flow of finance in a typical company.

We now look more closely at the five budget construction criteria. Limits will be quickly revealed and the formation of the final plan will normally take several movements through the company.

1 The boundaries for profit growth will be:
    Cash availability
    Market potential
    Plant, equipment and vehicle requirements
    The requirement, availability and calibre of human resources
2 The market potential will be outlined by:
    The existing business or, with acquisitions, previous history (as a guide and not just a basis for extrapolation)

166

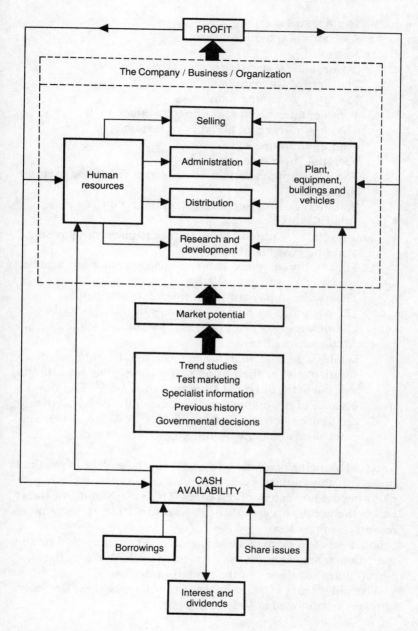

Figure 9 Company resource and finance flow

167

Trend studies
Specialist marketing studies
Test marketing
Governmental decisions
The state of trade cycles
The study of competition
3   Governmental decisions will directly affect:
Changes in levels of all types of taxation
Capital allowance rules
National Insurance contributions
The popularity of certain goods and services, for example
cigarettes
Pollution control and movement of certain goods
Other factors
4   The resource requirements within the time-scale envisaged
may not be possible, that is:
The ability to gain sufficient cash resources whether
borrowed or self generated
The ability to pay sufficient interest or dividends
The obtaining of human resources of the right skills
The obtaining of the plant, equipment and vehicles
5   Previous achievements:
While it is true that these must not be thought of as
straitjackets for the future, many companies find that to
step out of the old mould is almost impossible. This may be
because of the interactions of some of the points above, or
the desire not to take too much risk. A different management may well come to different conclusions.

Careful balancing of all the issues will now take place in the final
stages of the budget preparation. The process will include
planning the movement of resources. Those parts of the business
where the accent on growth is to be centred may receive more
resources, others less.

Some new parts may be created; others removed. For the
individual manager this is the moment of truth. What are the final
agreed plans for his bit of the overall budget?

We shall discuss how a manager can influence these decisions
after we have looked at time-scales.

How far ahead can a company budget?

We ought to take several views of the road ahead in a company. We ought to take a longish look, three to five years or longer. Even at three years the view will not be very clear, and at five years it will be distinctly misty! However there is little doubt that we should try to look that far ahead to set out our course. It is like a ship's journey. If there is no place to aim for, the journey will become a meandering path over the oceans. If a final goal exists, then all the intermediate planning and navigation is towards that goal. In business it helps the one and two year budgeting if there is a longer-term plan. Plans will change; no management however astute and skilled, can control external or even all internal circumstances. What they can do is to have alternative plans available to deal with such situations. The correct course is therefore to:

1 Set down a long-term plan
2 Detail intermediate plans within the framework of 1
3 Be ready for change

Budgeting is a live process. It is not something brought out of the cupboard once a year, dusted off, revamped and put back again. It is a continuous process. Businesses which plan and budget properly over as long a time-scale as practicable are more likely to succeed. One good reason is the simple truth that in carrying out such planning the business is being fully researched.

Your contribution to budgeting

The most important step will be to question what has gone before and not assume that to be a sacred criterion for the future. Your responsibility must always be to arrange your budget so that you get more results for less cost. Easy to say, not always to do, but new ways of achieving goals have to be continuously explored. For a start, do not assume that any merit rises for staff will automatically result in an increased budget. Look into the quality of the staff instead.

It is always essential to have able staff, who are well paid, and who will do a better job than a larger number of lesser quality people. This is especially true in high technology areas such as computer systems or design engineering. Additionally, it may be possible to employ more labour-saving machinery in place of staff, so that the discounted capital is less expensive than the previous payroll.

Productivity gains in two ways from a new, hard look at the staff in terms of value for money. Firstly, less total wages for the same output, or more relative output, means more profit. Secondly, encouragement for those who deserve it is likely to make them work better and the others strive a bit harder to obtain it. At this point it would be wrong not to mention that training or retraining may be an answer in some cases rather than completely disregarding your staff.

The general attitude outlined is, however, fairer to the majority, even if a small number have to suffer the results of their inadequacy. There may be other ways of solving the problem. Some departments may be understaffed or could use people who are not effective enough in other jobs. Natural wastage may take care of part of the problem. What is certain is that no good will come to the majority who work in a company if a minority are ineffective.

Business machinery, computers, robots and all forms of automation are not popular with those who may be affected. Man's ingenuity will not cease and more automation will follow. The budget is affected in three ways:

1 The cost of capital to buy equipment must be added to the budget
2 Some people will be unwanted and their pay will therefore be saved
3 New people will probably be required to operate new equipment, but in lesser numbers.

Will all this reduce the budget? It may do or it may give rise to increased sales or service for the same cost. The appropriate department of management has to assess carefully the effects, and budget accordingly.

We have emphasized the human effects of budgeting to show that budgets are not accountants' toys but the living being of the business. They affect humans greatly and humans can achieve much by using them. In these days of information technology and great stress on productivity, it is vital to understand what may be required in the way you budget. You can then play a significant part in your company, great or small, by using your budget as an instrument of innovation and change, to obtain better productivity, profitability and value for money.

Budgets in practice

We have discussed the philosophy of the budget and the human scene behind the budget, but what of the mechanics of budgeting, the task you will do? The budget may be large or small; the accounting system may be good or indifferent. From top management (probably advised by a budget committee) must come an initial framework. Suppose that in a manufacturing company there are directorates for the responsibilities and likely operating costs, stated as follows:

Engineering and manufacturing	£5m
Marketing and sales	£2m
Finance and administration	£1m
Personnel and training	£1m
Total operating cost	£9m

This initial budget will have been worked out in relation to likely turnover and profit levels, and all levels of management should have assisted in their respective directorates.

The total cash flow position may then look like this:

Budgeted surplus	£15m
Less operating cost	(£9m)
Less funding costs	(£1m)
Equals profit before tax	£5m

Once the grand plan is approved, the directors will be able to distribute the final budget allocations to the various levels of management.

With the budgets will come the agreed objectives – for example, sales manager district 'A': sales of £2m for his portion of the budget.

Detailing a budget

In the first phase of budget preparation, the board of the company has to obtain estimates of likely total operating expenditure based upon an agreed corporate policy. At a detailed level this may mean

171

that an engineering manager has to estimate the cost of design and development of a new product; a manufacturing manager the production engineering and manufacturing cost; and the sales manager selling cost. These estimates may represent the whole or part of the activities of the management concerned. The total budget formation is on a 'tree' basis as in Figure 10. A paricular company will have its own method of grouping these costs.

Other backing information would be used; for example, total salaries would stem from different grades and skills of individuals. The company could then not only find out about the monies involved, but would also be able to classify the types of skills needed in total.

Before you, as an effective manager, can prepare a budget, you will want to know and agree with your manager the goals you have to meet in the next budget period. This will enable you to plan to meet these objectives and the resource requirements. Although money is the end result, the value is built up from knowledge of resource requirements. You must fit your own type of business details to your budget, but, if you systematically go through your resource list and then think how you can obtain the greatest value for money throughout, you are more likely to produce an effective budget.

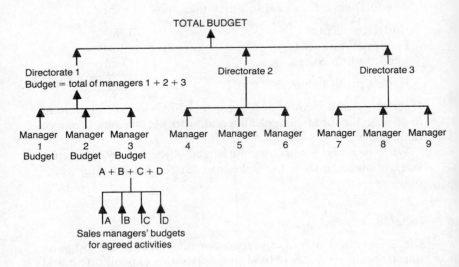

Figure 10   Total budget formation structure

172

The task, whatever it is, will require labour over the whole period. It may build up to a peak, particularly in the case of one-off jobs, or it may be a steady quantity, thus dictating to some extent the amount of work you could do. This is where innovation may pay dividends.

You may be able to increase your productivity by increased use of machines in one form or another; you may introduce more efficient working arrangements; or you may hire temporary labour to fill a peak demand if this is feasible. There may be other means which you consider advantageous.

How many people you need to do a job will be largely a question of past performance modified by future promise and ideas for improvement. Your industry averages should be known to you but beware that the comparison averages are really typical. Some grouping takes place in inter-firm comparisons. If the task is new and there are no criteria, then you have to use your skills, experience, common sense and value thinking to make a decision on your best estimates. You must also shop around for ideas.

You may have to consider the various overheads which come with the use of labour, such as National Insurance contributions, pensions, and the like. Usually these costs are given as an overhead proportion which you simply add on. It depends on the size of the business: large ones do this; smaller ones often require more detail.

Don't forget the other types of expenditure such as consumable items. It may be a small or a large amount – in a publications department, for example, there may be large expenditure on stationery and paper. Study existing budgets in your company and elsewhere, and make a comprehensive checklist. You may also have the added complication of land and buildings to consider, or it may only be office accommodation.

There may be charges levied by the company headquarters. These may be in the form of overheads, or you may have to do more work to calculate these. The composition of these could include rent for your premises, and services supplied to your department, for example drawing, copying or equipment depreciation.

Finally you may have to consider the outside purchases of material and equipment or the use of subcontractors.

Figure 11 shows how the budget is built up.

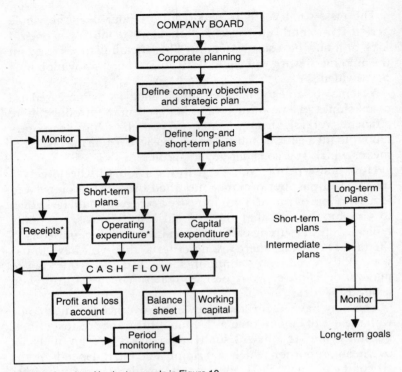

* Built up from 'tree' budget example in Figure 10

Figure 11   Budget formation

Rejection

What, unfortunately, often happens is that a budget is prepared in the usual way, after much passing of information on goals and likely budget totals, only to find that, when presented, it is rejected. Possibly the comment is 'Reduce by 10 per cent'. There can be two main reasons for this:

1   The company may overtrade without some cut in the overall budget and they are trying for a 10 per cent cut all round.
2   Your management may consider that you are too high by some amount, not necessarily 10 per cent, and are making you go through the budget again.

What do you do about it? Firstly, don't get all upset about the 'so and so' management above. Such action on their part is rarely nit-picking. Look further up through the company and you can imagine that the total of many sub-budgets, all a bit too high, can mean a lot when added together. Look upon it as a necessary fine-tuning exercise. You have only your budget to worry about!

Now go through every figure again. If, previously, you had to estimate a bit in one area or another, take a much closer look. Involve any necessary people in your department to look at their bit again. Have you put some contingencies in that have no real justification? Examine every item again with a view to reducing the budget by 15 to 20 per cent and see what it would do. How near to your goals could you get? If in the end you have managed to cut your budget by 5 per cent, and any further cuts would affect your goals, then re-submit and say so in a clear manner. Be sure you can justify all the thinking behind your final attempt.

You may find that this second attempt is accepted. If more savings are required, however, it may be 'cuts all round', or the cuts may be selective, including your budget. You will then have to see how such a reduction will affect:

1 Staff
2 Goals

In both cases you should put up a clear report on the effects, so that management is fully aware of the situation.

It is a fact, which sometimes seems unfortunate, that budgets are a compromise between what we would like and what we can have.

The effects of inflation

Throughout the Western world there is a general acceptance that inflation is bad, and efforts are made to contain it. We should be aware of the problems it causes in budgeting. It is only too easy to allow for inflation by 'upping' all estimates by the inflation index. This is patently wrong, as not all costs go up by the same amount. Two examples are oil and electronic equipment. Oil costs increased out of all proportion to the prevailing rate of inflation and dragged inflation up to new high levels, from which countries have been trying to escape for some years. On the other hand, the power/usefulness/price ratios of electronic equipment have tumbled and still continue to do so.

A company must proceed on the basis that the actual effect on costs must be estimated part by part, and no general increases allowed. The question of labour costs is difficult because of the pressure from labour groups (and they have a point), that their wages must:

a   not fall in relative terms because of inflation effects on the cost of living.
b   increase to give a better standard of living.

The company, on the other hand, has to look at its competitive position and its desire to contain unit costs (and it has a point, too, otherwise jobs may be lost as well as profit). Budgeting, therefore, is even harder under inflation conditions, especially when a large staff is involved. It can be seen that the pressure is even greater to substitute equipment for staff, provided the investment is soundly based.

17 Evaluating investment opportunities

Why evaluate?

The evaluation of investment opportunities is an area in which frequent and costly errors are made. There is pressure to increase productivity in the new industrial revolution of today. This, coupled with the speed of technological advance and the ever-present competition, means that companies have to constantly make and remake investment decisions, if profits are to be maintained and improved. Some of these decisions deal with projects spanning many years ahead.

The oil industry is the most quoted example of very large investment made well before any likely return – in other words there is a negative cash flow for perhaps several years. Other examples include power stations and mining. The analysis of such projects calls for wise judgements involving many experts.

We do not all have oilfields to discover and exploit, but, whatever our capital expenditure plans, we should learn to apply sound rules for assessing the worth of that expenditure.

The four factors which should influence our decision are:

1 Technical knowldge of the end effect of the investment – more widgets per hour, cheaper production, increased production, new production, or advantageous displacement of manpower.
2 The real cost of the investment and its long-term benefits.
3 The comparison of this investment against others which apparently have an equal priority.
4 The timing of the purchase. Interest rates and resale values may have a bearing on this.

Analysis of all of the facts is vital because unused and/or unprofitable fixed assets are a drag on a business. Cash tied up in a venture could be critical and easily cause a company to fail. In this chapter we deal with the real cost of investment. For many years there have been two popular methods of looking at the viability of investment decisions. We will first give examples of these and point out certain weaknesses. They do give some indication of the benefit or otherwise of a particular capital project which explains the popularity of these methods over the years.

Payback (PB)

This is a simple method of looking at expenditure on, say, the purchase of machine tools, or other capital goods where there is a measurable advantage in the use of the equipment. We can calculate the number of years over which the project can earn enough to pay for itself.

Case 1 (PB)

A machine tool costs £2000. It will enable economies in production of £400 per year to be made. The payback is 2000 divided by 400 = 5 years.

Case 2 (PB)

The design and development of a new typewriter will cost £200,000. The estimated sales will provide profits of £15,000 in the first year, £40,000 in the second, £60,000 in the third and £85,000 in the fourth year. The payback period is 4 years since the profits amount to £200,000 in 4 years. Any real profit would be made after this, but, as we shall see later, the picture is much less clear than this.

Case 3 (PB)

A similar development costs £215,000 but no profit would be made in the first year. In the second year £10,000 profit is estimated, in the third year £40,000, in the fourth year £70,000, in the fifth year £70,000, and in the sixth year £25,000. The payback period on this basis is 6 years.

If we have to decide on the basis of the payback method between Cases 2 and 3, we would have to choose 2 because it gives a shorter period.

However, suppose the choice is between completely dissimilar

178

methods of achieving an end result, where perhaps the payback method can be more easily seen to be of lesser importance than judgement of a political nature.

Case 4 (PB)

A new underground railway will cost £60m and recover its cost in 8 years, the trains lasting about 20 years.

An alternative is a fleet of buses costing £9m where the cost is recovered in 2 years and the buses last about 2 years.

To say that the buses should be used because the payback period is only two years is plainly only looking at one issue.

Environmental factors, convenience and the possibility of growth are but three other general considerations. Apart from these, although the payback period is shorter for the buses, the question of early replacement must be considered.

The payback method is useful where income or savings may be cut prematurely. The disadvantages are:

- The actual profitability is not made clear. Although minimum payback time is an advantage, the object must be to increase profitability.
- The timing of expenditure and receipts is not taken into account. Whether funds have to be used from internal resources or borrowed, a minimum return must be made and timing of cash flows would have an important bearing on this.
- The cash flows occurring after the payback period are not used in the method, so we could have large cash flow movements which apparently do not matter.
- Confusion exists where negative cash flows occur unevenly before the period under measurement.

It would seem that the case against the payback method of investment appraisal is so strong that it should not be used. However, the method could be a guide in eliminating projects with a payback period of, say, over five years. This, combined with a target return of 25 per cent, and assuming even cash flows, could adjust the five years downwards to three years. The method could be used in this way as a kind of net to catch those projects not complying with the rules.

Rate of return (RR)

This assesses the return on capital as an average percentage per annum of income less depreciation (average per year) divided by capital cost.

Case 1 (RR)

If the start-up capital for a project is £1000, income over 5 years is £450 per year and depreciation is 20 per cent of initial capital per year, then the net income is £450 − £200 = £250 per year.

$$\text{Rate of return} = \frac{250}{1000} \times 100 = 25\%$$

This is a simple case. What if the income varies each year? We could average out the incomes and calculate an average RR. The capital too could vary, in that it may be injected at more than one time in the life of the project. Averaging would again have to be done.

One of the worst features of RR is its inability to show that the normal delay between the initial investment and consequent income is affecting the choice of investment. This initial delay could clearly affect the rate simply because no income is earned in the early years. Comparison using the RR figure is difficult as the example in Table 6 shows.

Case 2 (RR)

We see in the following examples that the same RR is calculated, although the cash flows are different. Which would you choose? It is a difficult choice but we might be influenced by the fact that in project XYZ we get some real income in year 2, whereas in ABC we are still paying out in year 2, with no actual return until year 4. Can the business afford to wait for four years? If the money was borrowed would the cost of borrowing against the return be sensible?

In summary, the disadvantages of RR are:

- The method does not take account of time and its effect on money as well as the rate of return.
- Additional capital injection and current expenditure cannot be readily included.

Table 6 *Rate of return investment comparison*

Project ABC: initial capital = £10,000

| | Years | | | | |
	1	2	3	4	5
Income £	nil	nil	2,000	5,000	18,000
Less depreciation 20% per year	2,000	2,000	2,000	2,000	2,000
Net income	−2,000	−2,000	nil	3,000	16,000

Total net income = −£4000 + £19,000 = £15,000
Average net income = £3000 per year
RR = 3000/10,000 × 100 = 30 per cent

Project XYZ: initial capital = £10,000

| | Years | | | | |
	1	2	3	4	5
Income £	nil	3,000	5,000	9,000	8,000
Less depreciation 20% per year	2,000	2,000	2,000	2,000	2,000
Net income	−2,000	1,000	3,000	7,000	6,000

Total net income = − £2000 + £17,000 = £15,000
Average income = £3000 per year
RR = 3000/10,000 × 100 = 30 per cent

- As in the payback method, negative and 'after the event' cash flows cannot be properly incorporated.
- The timing of cash flows is not weighted in any way.

Discounting techniques

If you invested £100 in a building society at the start of the year, you would expect to receive at the end of the year your £100 plus interest at the prevailing rate. At 7 per cent you would have £107 invested at the end of the year. Suppose, instead of that

181

arrangement, you wanted to have £100 at the end of the year, then you would need to invest $100/(1 + I)$ where I is the current rate of interest. At 7 per cent, as before, the initial sum would be £93.46.

Now if someone owed you £100 and did not pay for a year, then, at 7 per cent, the repayment at that time would only be worth £93.46. Discounting money to be received in the future is an essential item in the comparison of investment. It enables the calculation of what we shall call Net Present Value or NPV.

The assumption of an interest rate depends on whether the money for the capital expenditure is borrowed from a bank or similar institution, raised from share sales, or raised from surplus funds held in the business which may or may not already be invested. Taxation effects or grants of one kind or another may further complicate the position.

Closely related to NPV is Discounted Cash Flow or DCF.

Example 1

For an outlay of £950, which we borrow at 10 per cent interest (on the reducing balance of the loan principal), we can buy some equipment which saves £300 per year in production costs. How long will it take to get the £950 back? Interest is calculated at yearly intervals. Taxation effects are excluded and the equipment resale value can be ignored. A table is constructed showing the cash flows. See Table 7.

By adding 10 per cent interest to the reducing capital sum each

Table 7   *Example 1*

Years	Initial or balance of capital to be paid back	Interest at 10%	Revenue savings from use of machine	Net balance Col. 1 + Col. 2 − Col. 3
1	950	95	300	745
2	745	75	300	520
3	520	52	300	272
4	272	27	300	−1

182

year, and taking into account the £300 saving, the balance of capital is extinguished at the end of year 4 (except for −£1 which we can ignore). We can thus afford to borrow money at 10 per cent (termed the DCF interest rate) to carry out this project over a four-year period, but with no profit.

If the −£1 had been a large negative value, it would have meant that the DCF rate could have been higher, which in turn would mean a real profit over the bank or other borrowing rate. The 'over-succeeding' case is important because one of the criteria in the investment appraisal may be to choose a number of years in which projects have to achieve a given DCF rate.

Example 2

Calculate the DCF rate of return on the following project:

1	Development costs	1st year	£25,000
2	Manufacturing costs	2nd year	£40,000
3	Sales revenue	2nd year	£10,000
4	Manufacturing costs	3rd year	£40,000
5	Sales revenue	3rd year	£80,000
6	Manufacturing costs	4th year	£40,000
7	Sales revenue	4th year	£80,000

Project closes at end of 4th year

To illustrate the movement of cash flows, we lay out yearly figures and choose interest rates of 10 per cent and 20 per cent for easy calculation, see Table 8. In the 20 per cent column we finish up with a negative balance, which means that we could have had a figure slightly higher than 20 per cent. If the actual cost of borrowing or the loss of other investment was, say, 10 per cent, then the project would make 10 per cent overall profit, after taking the interest charge into account.

We have been inexact on three main counts:

1 The exact figure in lieu of 20 per cent has not been found
2 We have used a year as an interval, whereas income is coming in during years 2, 3 and 4 and thus the interest will be less
3 We have ignored taxation effects including grants and allowances

The laying out of a table, as above, where interest values are added is not difficult. There are, however, standard tables from which

183

Table 8 *Example 2*

Interest rates	10%	20%
Development costs (1st year)	£25,000	£25,000
+ interest year 1	2,500	5,000
	27,500	30,000
+ manufacturing costs (2nd year)	40,000	40,000
	67,500	70,000
− sales income (2nd year)	(10,000)	(10,000)
	57,500	60,000
+ interest year 2	5,750	12,000
	63,250	72,000
+ manufacturing costs (3rd year)	40,000	40,000
	103,250	112,000
− sales income (3rd year)	(80,000)	(80,000)
	23,250	32,000
+ interest year 3	2,325	6,400
	25,575	38,400
+ manufacturing costs (4th year)	40,000	40,000
	65,575	78,400
− sales income (4th year)	(80,000)	(80,000)
	−14,425	−1,600

discounted values can be taken. They usually show the value of £1
at different rates of interest and over varying number of years, see
Table 9. The construction of a small table is not difficult using a
pocket calculator. Taking the 8 per cent set as an example:

$$\text{Year } 1 = \frac{1}{1.08} \quad \text{Year } 2 = \frac{1}{(1.08)^2} \quad \text{Year } 3 = \frac{1}{(1.08)^3} \quad \text{Year } 4$$

Table 9 *Discounted values of £1*

| Years | Discount factors | | | | | |
	7%	8%	9%	10%	11%	12%
1	0.9346	0.9259	0.9174	0.9091	0.9009	0.8928
2	0.8735	0.8573	0.8417	0.8264	0.8116	0.7971
3	0.8164	0.7938	0.7721	0.7512	0.7312	0.7117
4	0.7630	0.7350	0.7083	0.6829	0.6587	0.6354

Table 10 *Example 3*

Years	Net revenue	8% discount factors	DCFs at 8%	12% discount factors	DCFs at 12%
1	300	0.9259	278	0.8928	268
2	300	0.8573	257	0.7971	239
3	300	0.7938	238	0.7117	213
4	300	0.7350	220	0.6354	191
		Total	993	Total	911

Example 3 (based on Example 1)

This time we will use tables to find the present values of the revenue savings and we choose 8 per cent and 12 per cent to show two answers which will be either side of the previous result which was 10 per cent. See Table 10.

When we subtract the final value of the discounted positive cash flow from the original capital cost we get:

at 8%   £950 (original capital outlay) less £993 = −£43
at 12%   £950 less £911 = +£49

Thus 8 per cent is not enough and 12 per cent is too much. Interpolation, assuming a linear relationship, gives:

8% + 43/92 × (12% − 8%) = 9.87, or approximately 10% as before

Another way of looking at the problem is to split the capital and revenue and perform separate calculations based upon a rate of interest, say 10 per cent. The capital is first depreciated over the term involved, 4 years in this example. Using sinking fund tables, we find that to depreciate £950 over 4 years at 10 per cent, the multiplying figure is 0.21547, that is, £950 × 0.21547 = £204.7. This is the sum we would have to put away each year to provide 'new' capital, taking into account the compound interest effect of 10 per cent on the 'building up' amount.

The annual income (savings on production costs) is £300 less the capital depreciation of £204.7 = £95.3

$$95.3 \text{ (the effective income)} \times \frac{100}{950} = 10\% \text{ (approx.) which is the result we had before}$$

The DCF method is very similar to a building society repayment mortgage, where a rate of interest is calculated, designed to give a payment amount that clears interest and capital over a certain number of years. This is the true rate of return on the outstanding capital.

The NPV method looks either at the net present value itself as an indicator of the effect of time, or assumes a rate of interest below which a company would not accept a project. By taking the positive cash flows, discounting them at the chosen rate of interest (to obtain NPVs) and subtracting the total of these from the original capital, a positive, zero or negative amount will remain.

Example 4

The capital for a project is £2000, the acceptable rate of interest for NPV calculation is 12 per cent, the positive cash flows are £700 per year for 5 years.

Because the cash flows are all the same, we can avoid drawing up a table by using a formula. The example given earlier in respect of 8 per cent can be put into a general form by the following (where P = present value, A = value before discounting, r = rate of interest, and n = number of years):

$$P = \frac{A}{(1 + r)}$$

$$NPV = \frac{700}{1.12} + \frac{700}{(1.12)^2} + \frac{700}{(1.12)^3} + \frac{700}{(1.12)^4} + \frac{700}{(1.12)^5} - 2000 \text{ (original capital)}$$

$$= 625 + 558.0 + 498.2 + 444.9 + 397.2 - 2000 = 523$$

As the result is positive, that is, a higher rate of interest could have been successfully used, then, if the minimum rate was 12 per cent, the project should be accepted.

The assumption in these cases is that funds are available or can be obtained.

In conclusion:

- NPV and DCF do take the value of money in the future properly into account.

- These methods are not, however, the whole story, merely a tool to be used correctly: they cannot relieve the entrepreneurial decision-maker of his judgement.
- It may be necessary in some cases to use intervals of less than a year in order to make the calculations more accurate.
- The inclusion of taxation effects, estimated reliefs for capital allowances, reliefs from corporation tax in a project's current expenditure, and other factors, can all be included in the calculation of DCF and NPV. The timing of such entries is obviously important.
- The subject of capital expenditure and its treatment is a complex one. We have introduced the subject and suggest that the reading list at the end of this book will provide more detailed information.

PART 5

Managing information

Managing Information

18 Your own deskmate

Micro possibilities

The office micro is the spearhead of the information technology revolution. It may take the form of a terminal on the manager's desk connected to other terminals, databases, and mainframes in a corporate network. It may take the form of a stand-alone micro on his desk. It may be a word processor on the secretary's desk.

Whatever form a micro takes, we are dealing with the same general type of equipment. It is one which every modern manager needs to know about and to understand. In principle, the home computer is the same as the office micro, though usually with fewer facilities. As the prices of home computers start at less than £50, a manager can buy his own home computer and learn a great deal from it. For £400 or less you can buy a home computer on which you can perform a whole range of tasks such as:

- Work out the impact of interest rate changes on your mortgate repayments.
- Calculate the likely outcome of savings, insurance, and pension schemes using compound interest.
- Plan and monitor your personal budget and cash flow.
- Maintain a database of names, addresses, phone numbers and birthdays.
- Perform simple word-processing jobs such as producing a batch of change-of-address letters.
- Study a subject for which there are computer training programs – for example, learn the use of a computer language such as BASIC.
- You could also take some work home and use the computer to help you solve a business problem or uncover a business opportunity; we mention some examples of this later.

191

The microcomputer

The elements of a microcomputer can be divided into:

Hardware
Software
Support

The office micro is essentially a tool for solving business problems. As a manager, you should be concerned with what your micro will do for you rather than with the technical details of the micro itself. It does help to have a superficial knowledge of the technicalities and so we cover these briefly in the next few pages.

Hardware

The hardware of any computer consists of a means of putting information into it, a main memory to hold immediate information, a backing store to hold large amounts of information not currently being processed, a processing unit, and a means of output. The modern business micro comes in an integrated unit with the following main hardware elements:

1   *A keyboard* to input information. In some cases this is linked to the micro by a flexible cable so that it can be placed conveniently for use.

2   *The central processing unit or CPU.* This is the 'brains' of the micro and handles all the processing as well as controlling the micro.

3   *The monitor, Visual Display Unit, or VDU.* This is used to display information on the screen. Input that is keyed in via the keyboard is usually displayed on the VDU so that it can be checked as it is entered. Results of calculations made by the micro, and information selected from its memory or backing store can also be displayed. Some micro VDU screens can be tilted and swivelled to provide easy viewing. VDU displays can be in a single colour or in several colours. To keep the costs of home computers down, a domestic TV set is often used as the monitor.

4   *The ROM or Read Only Memory.* This memory holds control information for the micro, in particular it holds the sequence of instructions to be followed when the micro is switched on.

The user can only read information from the ROM. You, as a user, cannot write into the ROM and hence you cannot overwrite or corrupt the control information.

5   *The RAM or Random Access Memory* provides temporary storage. It is used to hold programs or parts of programs that the micro is currently obeying, together with the information that the micro is processing.

6   *The backing store* provides a permanent store for programs and data. Data, incidentally, is the computer jargon term for information – other than program instructions – processed by a computer. There are several different forms of backing store. The most common on the office micro are the floppy disk and the fixed disk, which is often referred to as a Winchester disk. On home computers the cheapest backing storage medium is the cassette, similar to an audio cassette.

The floppy disk unit is like a record player which plays disks, except that it is used to record and play back data rather than music. The most common floppy disk in use at the time of writing is the 5¼ inch diameter disk, holding one megabyte of information. Other sizes and capacities are offered.

The floppy disk is important because it is a means of transferring both data and packaged programs into your micro without having to key them in via the keyboard. A library of floppy disks can be held and used in your micro as required. The disks themselves are relatively inexpensive.

The fixed disk is not interchangeable in the way that a floppy disk is. It does, however, provide a storage medium for large amounts of data – five and ten megabyte capacities are common.

We expect that other forms of backing store will become available over the next few years.

7   *The printer.* The monitor or VDU provides an instant picture of the information you need. In many cases you will also need a printed record of the output, either to hold for reference or because you want to send it to someone else not linked into your network. Printers of various kinds can be connected to your micro. The type of printer you select depends upon the quality of print and the speed of printing that you require. High quality correspondence printers are available for printing letters if you use your micro as a word processor.

8   *The input/output ports.* The number of peripherals (such as

193

printers and disk units) that you can attach to your micro is governed by the number of input/output ports on the machine. A communications port is necessary if you intend to link your micro to other micros or to connect it to a network.

Software

The software is the really important part of your micro. Without software your micro is useless. You must have an operating system in order to use your micro at all. The operating system which runs with your micro will determine what other programs you can use. All the other programs that you use, whether they be language compilers, utilities, or application programs, have to interface with the operating system. If your micro uses an operating system such as CP/M, then the range of programs that you can use will be very large. Another up and coming operating system is UNIX. With lesser known operating systems you may be very limited in the range of programs that you can use.

The programs which actually help you to solve your business problems are the applications programs. These are of two types – the bespoke or specially written program, and the packaged program. In a grey area between the two are some packaged programs designed to be tailored to the particular needs of an individual user.

Managers may decide to write their own bespoke programs or to employ a software house or independent consultant to do the work for them. This will be more time-consuming and expensive than buying a packaged program off the shelf, but it has the advantage that the program is tailored to solve your specific business problem.

Programs are available to help the manager – or software house – who wants to write his own bespoke application programs. There are language compilers which translate the 'high level' language used by the programmer into machine code, which your micro will understand. There is also a whole range of utilities to help with the task of developing effective programs.

The largest range of packaged application programs at the time of writing is probably that for use with the CP/M and (for multi-processors) the MP/M operating systems.

There are four broad categories of packaged software that will concern most managers:

- *Word processing*. Standard packages such as Wordstar are available. These are more than just a typists' package. They provide a wide range of facilities which are useful for editing reports, for inserting standardized paragraphs into sales proposals, for correcting letters without constant retyping, and for producing personalized mailshots.
- *Financial modelling*. Standard spreadsheet programs such as Calcstar and Visicalc provide a simple means of financial modelling. This is particularly useful for a branch manager or the owner of a small business. He can alter a single figure on which his budget or cash flow forecast is based – for example, he can alter the assumed margin on sales from 28½ to 29⅛ per cent – and the package will rapidly work through all the figures that are affected by this change. This can eliminate hours of boring and error-prone work. With your next year's budget forecast on a Calcstar spreadsheet, you can smile each time your boss comes back and alters one of the guideline assumptions.
- *Database or electronic filing system*. Packages exist to help you build up and organize a database of relevant information so that it is available for fast recall and updating.
- *Accounting*. A vast range of specialized packages exists to satisfy the specialist needs of particular trades and professions. 'Publisher' is a specialized trade package for publishers, covering invoicing, back ordering, sales ledger, credit control, stock, product costs, purchase accounting and nominal ledgers. 'Jeweller' is a specialized branch oriented system for retail jewellers, which provides complete stock and accountancy control. If you can name a particular type of business, there is almost certain to be a specialized program package to help address its business problems. A great advantage of such packages is that a reputable supplier will rapidly produce amended versions to take account of changes in the law. There is a wide range of scientific and engineering packages which help carry out standard procedures and calculations with great accuracy and rapidity. There are also useful packages that will convert tables of figures into graphs and other pictorial representations such as bar charts or pie charts.

Support

The remaining element – support – covers a multitude of services, which you will need with your business micro. The main items are:

Advice and guidance in the use of the micro and the software packages
Training
Manuals and user guides
Maintenance, spares, and repair service
Supply of materials such as floppy disks and print ribbons
Supply of additional software and hardware as required

All these support services should be available from the firm from which you buy your micro. When you finally reach the point of buying you should make sure that they will be available. Obtaining all your micro hardware, software and support from a single supplier or a one-stop computer centre can save a lot of hassle and need not restrict your choice. Most reputable traders will be able to supply the full range of items that you will need with your micro.

Choosing a micro

There are plenty of keen salesmen ready and willing to sell you the very latest in microcomputers, complete with the latest 'state of the art' features. Remember the old adage, *caveat emptor* – let the buyer beware'. Approach the purchase of a desk-top micro professionally, just as you would approach any other substantial purchase. Recognize that the determining factor in your choice may well be the availability of a particular applications package rather than technical hardware features.

We recommend that you go through the following stages in choosing your business micro:

- Learn about micros and what they can do for you.
- Find out what policies, if any, your company has for the selection and use of micros.
- Define what purpose your micro is to serve.
- Identify the software and other features your micro will need to serve your purpose.
- Identify suitable micros.
- Evaluate the cost of the alternatives available against the benefits they would bring.

If you think that a business micro could help you, the first thing to do is to find out more about them and what they can do. You might do this by attending a one-day 'hands-on' micro course or workshop. You could take a correspondence course run by a reputable institution such as the Open University. You might be more ambitious and buy your own home computer to learn on. We know of several managers who have set out to learn on their home micro and have achieved useful business results in the process. Here are the stories of three of them:

Bill, an area sales manager for a large carpet firm, used his home micro to record his salesmen's performance. At first he merely entered their period sales, totalled them, and sorted them into a 'by results' order. Then he added car running expenses, results by area, returns, and other relevant information. Soon he was able to produce several useful analyses which would have been very tedious and time-consuming to produce without the micro. As a result of this work, he was able to set new targets, change territory boundaries, cut the level of expenses, and increase turnover. He took about eight months to achieve this, gradually learning, experimenting and building on each success.

John, the manager of a buying department in a wholesale company, needed certain statistical information, which did not exist in the rather old fashioned firm which he had just joined. He had a home micro and decided to try some self help. He started with very simple data entry. Eventually he put together a program which produced the results he needed. He used these results to prepare a report showing how the company could increase its profit by about £1500 a year, by a change in buying patterns which would result in improved discounts from certain suppliers.

Angus, the young manager of a retail store, collected records on his home micro. These included buying patterns, busy periods, and the timing of outside events. He analysed these and put forward a plan to improve store operation, based on changes in store marketing and local advertising. It resulted in improved turnover and profit, as well as demonstrating that he was a go-ahead and innovative manager.

Once you have learned a little about micros and what they can do for you, you need to find out what your company's micro policy is.

In some large companies with a strong central DP department, all micros may be bought or specified centrally. In others there may be simple guidelines which you are expected to follow, such as 'All micros purchased must support CP/M and conform to the standards for Open Systems Interconnection.' Or the company may specify that all micros must be bought from a specific trader or manufacturer. In other companies, managers are only limited in their choice by normal budgetary or capital expenditure constraints.

Why do you want a business micro? Can you define the purposes for which you will use it? Be as precise as possible in defining these purposes and the workload involved. For instance, if you intend to use the micro for direct mail shots, how many names and addresses will you hold? Will they be coded so that only certain people receive particular mailings? How many letters will be produced each week? What is the minimum standard of print quality for those letters and what is the desirable standard?

What features will your micro need to do what you want? It is probably wise to start with the software. Are there any packages that will do what you require? If so, on which micros will they run? If you do not intend to use a package, which programming language will you use and what programming aids will you need?

Important hardware considerations will include:

Size of RAM
Amount of backing store needed
Quality and speed of printing
Monochrome or multi-colour VDU
Stand-alone or linking to a network
Expansibility

There are some less obvious considerations. There are hundreds of makers and suppliers of business micros. Some of these may offer a technically sound product but the firm itself may not be soundly based. Choose a micro which is made and supplied by a firm which is likely to stay in business for several years. Do not be tempted to buy some low price micro which is obsolescent or the product of a firm about to leave the market. Some quite substantial firms have pulled out of the micro business because of the fierce competition. A well established firm will supply all the support you need and still be in business when you need to extend your micro with additional hardware or software.

When you have identified the features that are important to you, it is sensible to list those which are essential and to rank the remainder in order of priority. List the micros that would meet your requirements. Then go to visit some users of those micros and discuss with them their experience of using the micro. Try to find out if the micro has any drawbacks before you buy. Check, for instance, whether there are any special environmental requirements. There shouldn't be, as most modern micros are designed for use in an office environment.

The next stage is the financial evaluation. Here you should look at the total cost of ownership. The hardware cost is likely to be less than half of this.

Some traders will sell you a package which includes the operating system and maybe some standard package programs, such as a spreadsheet and word-processing package. They may even offer a complete hardware and software package, tailored to your trade, for an inclusive price. If the hardware and software are not bundled into a single price, you will find that the software price can be relatively high as you increase the amount you buy. A large company may achieve significant savings as a bulk purchaser.

Another significant item in your total cost of ownership is your maintenance contract. You should, incidentally, look for an assurance that maintenance and spare parts will be available for at least five years. If they are not, you could face a costly early replacement.

Finally, compare the costs of your micro with your estimate of the benefits. In a great many cases the result will favour going for a micro. You will be taking a positive step to derive benefit from the new information technology.

19 Data protection and privacy

Why?

Why should any manager be interested in data protection and privacy? Surely this is a matter for the experts – the DP manager and the company secretary?

This may once have been so, but two developments have changed this. A manager, in many countries including Britain and most Western European nations, has legal obligations in relation to data protection and privacy. You can suffer severe penalties for failure to observe those obligations.

Secondly, the explosive spread of terminals and personal computers on to the desks of managers and other office workers involves them directly in handling computer-based information, and potentially gives them rapid access to very large amounts of data. Much of the information is about individuals and would have a commercial value (if only as the foundation for a mailing list). Indeed there are some companies whose only material asset is the information they hold. An example is a credit rating company; another is a company such as Telerate which provides a Value Added Network Service (VANS). Admittedly, companies which provide VANS have computers, large numbers of terminals, and a network for gathering information, but their value lies in the information they hold and can provide. This information may be available in other ways to the public, but VANS may present it in a way that enables the subscriber to access the information he needs quickly and with confidence.

In fact, information is rapidly becoming an important commodity, traded in its own right. It is traded across international frontiers. Different countries have different laws governing the protection of data and of individual privacy. 'Encryption' is a standard method of protecting highly sensitive information and is widely used. There are, however, some countries where it is illegal to import or export encrypted data.

The concept of a right to privacy is not something new that arrived with the information technology age. In 1888, Judge Cooley of the USA defined privacy as 'the right to be left alone'. The definitions have become more sophisticated since then, but the basic principle of privacy is claimed as a fundamental human right. This has led to the production of guidelines on data protection by the Organisation for Economic Co-operation and Development. A Council of Europe Convention for the protection of individuals with regard to automatic processing of personal data has been signed by fifteen European nations, and ratified by several countries including France and Sweden.

It was always relatively easy to break into an office and abstract information from a filing cabinet. You probably did not even need to break in. All that was needed was a little co-operation from a clerk, secretary or cleaner. Photography and photocopiers made the abstraction of information from manual files even easier.

At first sight, the IT revolution has made computer-stored information more vulnerable. Much more information is stored in a single place. Modern disk stores can hold hundreds of millions of words in the space of a cubic metre. Modern databases link information together so that it is easy to access all the information held in a database about an individual, a firm, or a product. There has been an inevitable tendency to collect information for one specific purpose and then to find that it can be profitably used for another, or that the aggregation of information collected for several specific but different purposes becomes valuable in itself.

Where individuals are concerned, for instance, information collected for any purpose may be helpful in assessing credit-worthiness or suitability for employment or promotion.

Fears have also arisen in connection with government use of computers. Will computers owned by different government departments talk to each other and compare or combine information held about specific firms or individuals? Given that knowledge is power, many people fear that this would greatly increase the power of the police and tax authorities. There has in the past been a degree of confidentiality implicit in the dealings between an individual or firm and their professional advisers. There have been fears that information given to a doctor in confidence could be made more widely available. This could, for instance, lead to problems with the individual's employer or could, in an extreme case, make blackmail possible.

The old proverb 'Give a dog a bad name' is appropriate to this discussion because computers also make it possible to retain information for a long time and still have instant access to it. Thus there have been fears that information about minor indiscretions, or even a criminal conviction when a teenager, might be readily available to an employer thirty years later, or revealed to all the world in a newspaper comment. Fears of this sort may seem irrational and you may well say that the innocent have nothing to fear. Yet there are few among us who have lived a totally spotless life.

Strangely enough, the introduction of computers into the police may have had the opposite effect. The law requires that certain criminal convictions are deleted from the records if no further conviction is recorded within a specified period of time. Under the old manual systems, this weeding of the records was sometimes haphazard, and the records were often not purged of these time-expired convictions. This was not a malicious contravention of the law but arose from the inherent difficulty of manipulating manual records. With computers it is a simple matter to instruct the computer to search a file and delete all records where the last entry is over five years old.

There is no doubt that positive action is necessary in the information age to safeguard privacy and to ensure the protection of data. The law plays some part in this, particularly in relation to issues of privacy. Normal commercial self-interest also plays a large part in ensuring attention to the security of data.

The Data Protection Act 1984

In the United Kingdom, the law relating to data protection is incorporated in the Data Protection Act 1984. The Data Protection Registrar is appointed under the authority of this Act. He maintains a register of data users (and of computer bureaux). Only individuals or firms which have registered as data users may hold personal data on a computer. We use the term 'firm' loosely as it includes any organization. There are some specific exceptions, and there is a transition period during which the Act comes fully into force. However, if you hold any information about individuals on your computer – even on your micro or word processor – you will be well advised to study the full text of the Act or to obtain competent advice on it.

The definition of 'personal data' is fairly wide. It means 'data consisting of information which relates to a living individual who can be identified from the information (or from that and other information in the possession of the data user), including any expression of opinion about the individual but not any indication of the intentions of the data user in respect of that individual'.

If the Data Protection Registrar refuses to register a firm as a data user or deletes it from the register, this could have very serious implications for the firm. There is a Data Protection Tribunal to which such a firm can appeal.

The Data Protection Act incorporates seven principles relating to personal data held by a data user, and a further principle which also applies to data in respect of which services are provided by people running computer bureaux. These principles are:

1   'The information to be contained in personal data shall be obtained, and personal data shall be processed, fairly and lawfully.'

    For instance, you must not obtain information deceitfully. To ring up Mr Smith's bank and obtain details of his bank account by posing as Mr Smith would breach this principle.

2   'Personal data shall be held only for one or more specified and lawful purposes.'

    The key point here is that the purpose must have been registered with the Data Protection Registrar, who has powers to refuse registration in certain circumstances.

3   'Personal data held for any purpose or purposes shall not be used or disclosed in any manner incompatible with that purpose or those purposes.'

    This is the heart of the matter. Whenever you use or disclose information which your computer holds about individuals, you need to consider whether you are breaching this principle.

4   'Personal data held for any purpose or purposes shall be adequate, relevant and not excessive in relation to that purpose or those purposes.'

    This is straightforward. No doubt the limits of what is

203

'adequate, relevant and not excessive' will be defined by case law in due course.

5 'Personal data shall be accurate and, where necessary, kept up to date.'

This is obviously both desirable and difficult to achieve. There are some escape clauses, such as if inaccurate data have been received from the person concerned. However, it is clear that high standards of accuracy are now required.

6 'Personal data held for any purpose or purposes shall not be kept for longer than is necessary for that purpose or those purposes.'

This should help reduce the cost of archive storage!

7 'An individual shall be entitled –
   a at reasonable intervals and without delay or expense –
      (i) to be informed by any data user whether he holds personal data of which the individual is the subject; and
      (ii) to access to any such data held by a data user; and
   b where appropriate, to have such data corrected or erased.'

If a firm becomes the target of an active pressure group this could become a source of considerable aggravation.

8 'Appropriate security measures shall be taken against un-authorized access to, or alteration, disclosure or destruction of, personal data, and against accidental loss or destruction of personal data.'

Most data processing departments are already very security conscious. The real danger probably lies in the security of floppy disks for the word processor or desk-top micro. Another area to watch is the disposal of old computer printouts.

In addition to these principles the Secretary of State has authority under the Act to modify or supplement these provisions to provide further safeguards in relation to information about:

racial origin
political, religious, or other beliefs
physical or mental health or sexual life
criminal convictions

Your responsibility

Data protection and privacy is a new and important element in the life of the manàger. If you have any responsibility for information about people, and if you hold that information on a computer, you will be well advised to study the matter further.

20 Trends and statistics

Forecasting is not an exact science. This is something we should all remember when we try to use a statistical approach to a problem. However, statistical help is an essential part of the armoury that managers must have to help them make decisions in solving problems, including sales and stock demand trends, staff grading, and quality control. It is likely that the higher the management position the greater will be the effect of the decision. It is also likely that the more appropriate the aids that are used the better will be the forecasting.

One danger in all forecasting is that there is a tendency to use the results which are most convenient and which fit preconceived ideas. As a manager, we can learn ways of manipulating information by statistical methods, but we must take into account that the weighting of information is as important as the method. Changes in conditions or seasonal variations can make some results meaningless if not allowed for.

The other important point is that the likelihood of one answer in forecasting being the only one is not high. Although the idea is not popular in some management circles, it is better to point out the most and least likely possibilities so that planning can contend with the situation. It may be that eventually someone has to choose one course, but full information is essential. Even the final decision can be subject to a statistical approach if there are sufficient grounds.

Moving averages

One common demand is some means of detecting the trend in, say, a series of sales figures. The need for this may arise either in estimating future sales or in forecasting a stockholding such that no severe under- or overstocking takes place.

Table 11 *Moving averages*

Month	Sales £000s	Cumulative total	Moving average (nearest whole number)
1	100	100	100
2	70	170	85
3	90	260	87
4	110	370	85
5	90	460	92
6	120	580	97
7	110	690	99
8	130	820	103
9	120	940	104
10	140	1080	108

Table 11 lists monthly sales for a sports wholesale company and, by adding each subsequent month's sales to the last addition and dividing by the number of months gone, will give a simple moving average which notes the trend from the start of the figures.

Figure 12 plots the sales and moving average. The latter smooths out the irregular sales figures but is moving well behind the actual sales. It would be possible to take a general line through the moving average and calculate future sales figures, but, just as the moving average smooths out the sales variations, so a multiplier effect would operate the other way.

To illustrate this, let us look at two interpretations of the continuation of the moving average.

First, continuing the moving average line, it look as if month 11 is 110, month 12 is 115 and month 13 is 120. The possible sales figures are shown in the first part of Table 12.

Second, continuing the moving average line, it looks as if month 11 is 110, month 12 is 113 and month 13 is 115. The possible sales figures are shown in the second part of Table 12.

The variations in the results from merely looking down the line of the moving average and seeing a different trend show the danger in working backwards from the moving average. The moving average is simple to use and does give a trend line, but it lags behind the recent events because it has all the previous figures averaged into it.

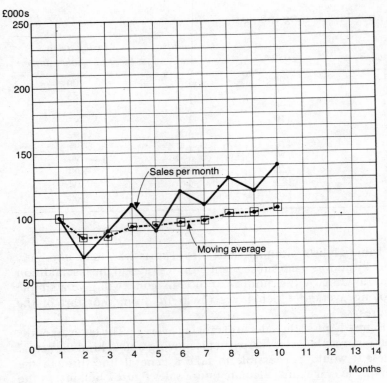

Figure 12 Sales per month (showing moving average)

Table 12

Month	Moving average	Moving average × months = cumulative total	Less previous cumulative total	Sales
11	110	110 × 11 = 1210	−1080	130
12	115	115 × 12 = 1380	−1210	170
13	120	120 × 13 = 1560	−1380	180
11	110	110 × 11 = 1210	−1080	130
12	113	113 × 12 = 1356	−1210	146
13	115	115 × 13 = 1495	−1356	139

208

Period moving averages (PMA)

This is a modification of the simple moving average whereby the average is moved over a chosen period of time. In this manner we are able to:

- Look at progress over a defined period such as one year, six months, etc.
- Choose periods that take into account seasonal changes.

The next table (Table 13) uses the same sales figures as before but averages them over three and six month periods. The moving total is the addition of the first three or six months plus the next month less the first month of the previous addition; for example, to calculate the eighth month of the six month set, the eighth month amount is added and the second month amount deducted (the first month is deducted when the seventh month is calculated). In the three month PMA, the moving totals are divided by three. In the six month moving total they are divided by six.

In Figure 13 the three and six month moving averages are plotted. The choice of period gives very different results. The three monthly moving average follows the sales figure, but avoids the extreme fluctuations while the six month moving average shows more clearly the general trend.

The moving total period can be chosen to start at a certain time of the year and encompass different periods.

Table 13

Month	Sales £000s	3-month moving total	3-month moving average	6-month moving total	6-month moving average
1	100	—	—	—	—
2	70	—	—	—	—
3	90	260	86.7	—	—
4	110	270	90.0	—	—
5	90	290	96.7	—	—
6	120	320	106.7	580	96.7
7	110	320	106.7	590	98.3
8	130	360	120.0	650	108.3
9	120	360	120.0	680	113.2
10	140	390	130.0	710	118.3

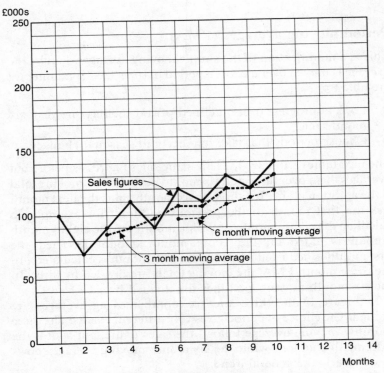

Figure 13   Sales per month (showing period averages)

It is still not possible to include weighting factors or to adjust the figures to get a better fit to the existing results, thus giving more confidence to predictions.

Exponential moving averages (EMA)

This is a popular method of detecting trends and estimating new results. There is the ability to obtain a close fit to previous information and, in the process, find a constant which can then be used for future estimation. The method gives confidence because of the controlled approach but, as in all statistical methods, there is no certainty about the future. There is, however, a larger degree of probability that the estimations will be nearer to the truth by

210

this method than by guesswork. This is another aspect of planning and there are few managers today who would argue against planning all tasks, large and small.

The basis of the EMA is the automatic adjustment of the new forecast by looking at previous success.

The full formula for calculation is a series (not often used complete):

$$F = \alpha S_0 + \alpha(1 - \alpha)S_1 + \alpha(1 - \alpha)^2 S_2 + \alpha(1 - \alpha)^3 S_3 + \text{etc.}$$

F = forecast for next period

S_0 = current period result

S_1 = last period result

S_2 = result of two periods ago

α = a constant. The value of this can be between 0 and 1 but is usually in the region 0.05 to 0.5. The effect of this constant will be shown later.

In order to simplify the method of use it can be shown that the full formula can be replaced by:

$$F = \alpha S_0 + (1 - \alpha)F_1$$

As an example:

F_1 = the forecast for this month's sales (made last month)
= 160

S_0 = the actual sales this month = 150

α = the constant, say 0.2 for this example

$F = (0.2 \times 150) + (1 - 0.2) \times 160 = 30 + (0.8 \times 160) = 158$

We can simplify the expression still further:

$$F = \alpha S_0 + (1 - \alpha)F_1 = F_1 + \alpha S_0 - \alpha F_1 = F_1 + \alpha(S_0 - F_1)$$
$$F = F_1 + \alpha \text{ (actual result less forecast)}$$

Checking this against the calculation above:

$$F = 160 + 0.2(150 - 160) = 160 - 2 = 158$$

It should be noted that the sign of the last expression is important and can be either positive or negative.

The higher the value of α the greater the effect recent results will have on the forecast. The lower the value of α the more the forecasts will follow the long-term trend. An example of two extremes can verify this.

Table 14

Month	Actual sales	Calculation for next month	Sales forecast
1	100		100
2	70	F = 100 + 0.8(70 - 100) = 100 - 24	76
3	90	F = 76 + 0.8(90 - 76) = 76 + 11.2	87.2
4	110	F = 87.2 + 0.8(110 - 87.2) = 87.2 + 18.3	105.3
5	90	F = 105.3 + 0.8(90 - 105.3) = 105.3 - 12.2	93.1
6	120	F = 93.1 + 0.8(120 - 93.1) = 93.1 + 21.5	114.6
7	110	F = 114.6 + 0.8(110 - 114.6) = 114.6 - 3.7	110.9
8	130	F = 110.9 + 0.8(130 - 110.9) = 110.9 + 15.3	126.2
9	120	F = 126.2 + 0.8(120 - 126.2) = 126.2 - 5	121.2
10	140	F = 121.2 + 0.8(140 - 121.2) = 121.2 + 15	136.2

Table 15

Month	Actual sales	$\alpha = 0.8$	$\alpha = 0.1$
1	100	100	100
2	70	76	97
3	90	87.2	96.3
4	110	105.5	97.7
5	90	93.1	96.9
6	120	114.6	99.2
7	110	110.9	100.3
8	130	126.2	103.3
9	120	121.2	105
10	140	136.2	108.5

Using the sales figures from Figure 12, inserting 100 as the first forecast (in the absence of other data), and taking $\alpha = 0.8$, we get the results shown in Table 14. Comparing these results with the actual and those using an α of 0.1 we get the results shown in Table 15.

Figure 14 has these results plotted on a graph and the effect of smoothing the constant α can be clearly seen.

This introduction to trend statistics will enable you to look at various trend figures and apply some sense to them. Methods of further adjustment to the errors in forecasts are available in order to increase accuracy. As they would occupy an undue share of the book, we suggest you consult the reading list at the end for more information.

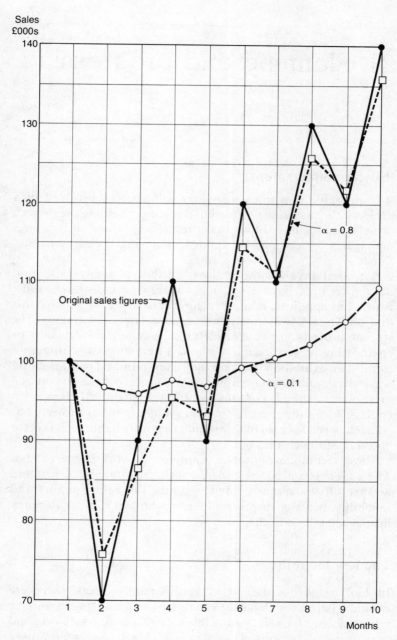

Sales £000s

Figure 14   Sales per month (showing exponential moving averages)

213

21 Planning and progressing

Project management

It is probable that most managers will become involved in a project either as a line or functional manager helping the project, or as a key member of a project team, or perhaps as a project manager. Projects may be defined as having a clear start and finish.

A project involves the pulling together of many skills and disciplines, often having tight time and resource constraints, and it is usual to appoint a manager whose sole task is to manage this one job. The task will involve much tactical decision making. The size of projects varies considerably. A small construction or engineering project, or moving into a new shop or setting up a stand at an exhibition may cost only a few hundred pounds. Build a motorway and you have millions of pounds at stake. In between these extremes the list of jobs requiring some overall direction is endless. From the need for overall management of projects has come the need for a set of techniques that will enable such tasks to be successfully carried out.

These techniques, however, apply to all work (more or less) where there is a need to define the task, set a time-scale, sort and arrange all the resources and optimize the value, quality and reliability. It is not surprising that a great deal of work in many businesses falls into this category.

The key techniques

In looking across the board at different projects, there are common points which have given rise to particular studies and the setting down of sensible guidelines. They are all based on good management disciplines and in our book *Successful Project*

Management (see reading list) we have suggested that it is useful to consider seven key techniques (or guidelines) in order to thoroughly plan and manage a project. Like many other such guidelines, once expressed they seem simple. Any difficulty, perhaps, is caused through carrying out less than thoroughly the suggested disciplines laid down.

1 Defining the project

The first of the key techniques is to define the project. It does not require much imagination to see that if we do not define what we are trying to do, we are unlikely to achieve it. In our experience, shared by many others in this field, a poor definition is often the first rock on which many an optimistic project has foundered. A whole series of questions must come to mind in trying to define a project. Take a relatively simple task of building a house or a bungalow. If you say to a builder 'Build me a house', what is he to do? He will want information on the type of house, size, number of rooms, what it must cost, what it must look like, where it is to be, and a hundred and one other details ranging from size of rooms to the colour of the paint. The house has to be defined in detail. Even if you buy a house already finished, someone must have defined it before it was built. Out of this simple example we can pick out certain issues that must pertain to other projects:

- What are we trying to do?
  - In this case build a house.
- What is the description of the project?
  - This is likely to consist of a simple description plus plans and specifications.
- How much must it cost?
  - Will we find all the money, or will we need a mortgage?
- How long will it take to build?
- What resources will be required?
  - In this case we subcontract to the builder.
- Are we getting the best value for money?
- How must it perform?
  - This is a function of the design, the position of the house, the comfort of the rooms (with items like central heating and air conditioning improving the comfort).
- How long must it last?

- This is determined by the quality of the design and the quality and reliability of all the parts.
- How can it be tested to see whether it performs properly?
  - Certainly parts of it can be tested and inspected as the house is built, like foundations and electrical and other services. The real test in this case will come from living in it for a few years.
- How can it be maintained?

Other questions that are not necessarily brought out in such a simple case as building a house, although they might apply, are:

- Is the project viable?
- What new design work is wanted?
- Do we need specialist advice and help?

Into definition must come a clear picture of the contractual responsibilities, which will bring out such things as performance, cost and guarantees. Are these normal to the industry at this time? Are any changes on the commercial front in prospect.

The object must be to continue to question, search and identify until we are satisfied that we have all the facts that are available at the time. We must identify all the key activities in the project. These are:

Performance
Specifications
Costs
Deliveries
Safety
Interfacing with other products
Reliability
Maintainability

Also under key activities will come knowledge of any technical barriers.

We must also identify the key decisions, for example:

Long-term delivery items to be ordered
Tooling to be ordered
Money at risk before contract (this sometimes has to happen in the real world)
Any money or resource commitment

In identifying such aspects of the project work, we must continue the search through experts, consultants, experience, writings and competitors until we have the planned measure of confidence.

While this is going on, there will, of course, be written documentation of the project definition in terms of:

Descriptions or plans of the key events and decision points
Lists
Specifications of end items and of the whole
Salient contractual points
Specifications to enable the items to be tested properly so that we know the performance can be achieved, and for operational use there will have to be maintenance arrangements and documentation.

In defining the project we are also using the results from the other six key techniques, which are:

2 Resources
3 Time-scales
4 Costs
5 Quality and reliability
6 Value optimization
7 Measurement and control

We shall discuss these separately, but the remaining activity in the definition is to be prepared for change. The definition will not stand still.

- *Requirements may change.* There may be a business takeover or a change of mind by the customer or of circumstances. Whatever the reason, we may have to change the definition.
- *Technology.* There may be a breakthrough and we are forced to investigate and/or use new methods, materials or items. Such changes can come about within our own company, through subcontractors, other companies or competitors.
- *The priority may change.* Other projects may become more important and cause cutbacks in yours, or there may be too many projects and some may have to be cut out altogether.
- *The business scene.* An example is the motor industry where changes in the law on safety belts, bumpers and exhaust fumes all caused definition changes in the motor car. Environment changes generally cause definition changes throughout industry. *We must be prepared!*

217

2 Resources

Key technique 2 concerns itself with resources of all kinds and includes:

FINANCE

Requirements for finance must be known from estimates and budgets. The provision of finance may involve work on loans, advance payments and special overseas problems. The cost of finance has to be known and the means of recovering it. The risk of the project must be weighed against the reward to help the financial decision. In looking at this, alternative actions should be considered. The cash flow of the project needs to be stated including the time-scales, amounts and break-even points.

HUMAN EFFORT

This concerns the types of effort:

- Physical, e.g. porters, labourers, carpenters, steelworkers, bricklayers, etc.
- Mental, e.g. clerks, engineers, programmers, etc.
- Male or female.
- Supervisory effort.
- Managerial effort.

MATERIALS AND EQUIPMENT

This ranges from raw material requirements to fully finished goods, and from consumable items like water, paper, oil, etc. to motors, cranes, diggers, tools, etc.

SPACE

We may need:

- Land on which to put new buildings or new arrangements within old buildings.
- Space to test something before sending to a customer.
- Special rooms for special tests.
- Rooms and offices for engineers and clerks.

SERVICES AND FACILITIES

These might well include:

- Tea.
- Gas, water, electricity, etc.
- A new road, port or airfield.

In key technique 2 there is nearly always a battle of compromise between what resources are desirable and what can be afforded. Time-scales are always too short and resources too few! Spare resources are nearly always needed, but nobody wants to pay for them. These are all the problems which must be consciously tackled under resources and, as far as is known at that stage, incorporated into the definition.

3 Time-scales

Key technique 3 is closely bound to resources, as immediately one is changed it has an effect on the other. This interaction is true of all the key techniques, but probably more immediately noticeable between resources and time-scales.

We have to formulate time-scales for all activities in a project: both to obtain resources, where there might be long delivery times, and to apply the resources. There will always be the conflict between being timely for the market-place or customer, and resource limitations, including cash, and design or ideas limitations. Sales lost early are rarely recovered in the later stages of selling a product, and the cash flow is not so favourable. There is a great deal you can do on any project by studying extremely carefully all activity time-scales and the logic of how these activities are best fitted together.

There are several ways of constructing and recording the information in order to have a master plan and then schedules of work, but, whatever method is used, the vital task is always to identify clearly at any time the *critical path*. The critical path is that path of activities through the project that will take more time than any other path.

There are two pitfalls to watch for in time-scale construction and consequent operation of the project. Optimism is a human weakness, so when estimates are received for activity times it is valuable either to know the person who is giving them and what his or her estimates are usually worth, or to double-check until you are reasonably sure the estimate is valid. The other pitfall is to economize on low-cost items on a critical path. This can easily be

219

penny wise and pound foolish. If the critical path lengthens, the project lengthens.

4 Quality and reliability

While these words have been largely applied to the manufacturing industry, they apply to all work, and here make up key technique 4. The quality and reliability of goods or services should not be a last minute thought, but must be built into those goods and services from the start. This is not a philanthropic gesture, for the consumer soon knows what goods or services to buy and buy again. Goods and services must be acceptable to a consumer at a price he or she is prepared to pay.

It is easy to think of the need for reliability in such ventures as space and air travel, where failure is usually disastrous for those involved. Reliability in weapons, motor cars, trains, etc. is also highly desirable. And we have all said rude things about the domestic items that refuse to work.

Quality is a little harder to define. It is concerned with looking good without shoddiness, having a marketing appeal, performing properly as it was intended to do. The length of time it performs properly brings us back to reliability. Quality is certainly not concerned with gold-plating everything – that would not improve the intrinsic quality of a bicycle. But if someone invented frictionless bearings for the wheels, that would be quality improvement.

The challenge with all quality and reliability questions is to achieve the necessary, acceptable standard at the lowest cost. It is fairly easy to achieve it with unlimited funds, but then the cost is so high that no one is going to buy the goods or services. Even if you have the best materials, best work and best appearance, without designed purpose, there is nearly always failure.

5 Costs

Without complicating the issue too much, it is a fact that *price minus cost equals profit*. This being so, then, to a large degree, profit on a project is within our grasp to control, provided that we can control the cost. This is key technique 5. There are two main facets in the costing process. If we are doing a project which is not producing a range of products, as would occur in, say, designing, developing and producing a new bridge or a custom built house, then the project cost is the same as the product cost and we are concerned with how much it costs to produce the one end item. The lower these costs, consistent with carrying out the specification, the more profit we shall make.

In the case of a project which is going to result in a range of products being produced – for example, designing, developing and manufacturing a new typewriter – there will be two distinct cost divisions. One, which in the end is likely to be the more important, is the cost of the typewriter itself, as this will dictate the profit we can make on our sale. The market-place usually dictates the selling price and, therefore, the profit is directly affected by the cost. The other cost facet is the cost of the design and development which may be amortized over the quantity of typewriters being made or, as in some large companies, it may simply be written off into the company's design and development overheads, which ultimately are written off in the total profit of the company. The important thing is that extra money spent in the project cost, that is the design and development, may in fact mean a greater profit if the product cost can be reduced substantially. It is, therefore, necessary to know how these project charges are to be written off, how much we can afford to spend in order to reduce the project cost and so on. The exact mechanics are outside the scope of this book, but if we can begin to think about this subject clearly, then we are halfway to the right solution.

One cost aspect which is often neglected is the feedback of all costs to designers from day one. It seems very obvious when you start to think about it: how can design A be compared to design B without knowledge of costs?

If we have a cost feedback system which is immediate and accurate, then we shall probably be pulling up by the boot straps all departments such as estimating, process planning, production engineering, value engineering, etc.

6 *Value optimization*

Value means different things to different people. A starving refugee would value a piece of bread highly; a slimmer not. Could there be a higher value placed on water than by someone lost in the desert? Whatever we do it has some value, and, in business, the higher the value consistent with demand and price, the more successful the article should be. This does not always follow, because the market-place is not perfect, but it is near enough to be taken as true.

To ensure that a product or a service is of high value, the examination of value needs to be started at the earliest possible stage. We are not just referring to manufactured items. If a store wants to be really successful, not only must the products be of good value, but the sales assistants should be taught their contribution to value in selling and serving the customers in an exemplary manner. Anything can be value-analysed, from a manufactured product to the performance of a computer programmer.

Value analysis is often confused with cost cutting. The big difference is that value analysis looks at function before anything else. Is there another way of doing the same job which makes it work better for the same price; the same performance at a cheaper price; or best of all better and cheaper? This may mean a completely different approach to how the problem was solved before. The biggest obstacle to improving value is a reluctance to look at new ideas. In the area of value analysis this reluctance is termed a 'roadblock'. Examples are:

'We can't take a chance on altering it'
'Our management would never allow it'
'It's been tried before'
'It costs too much'
'We're making a profit now'

Looking into value is rewarding. Our own experience is that it rarely fails. Value analysis should be employed:

● After training.
● With management backing.
● With a realization that people are inherently suspicious of change.
● By looking at the problem and not accepting old solutions as necessarily correct.

7 Measurement and control

We now come to key technique 7. As far as a project is concerned, unless there is continuous monitoring, measuring, feedback and control of all the functions appertaining to the project, there is little doubt that the project will be either ineffective or lead to disaster. An appropriate analogy is the ship's voyage. In the beginning, the voyage is planned and charted; in other words there is a master plan and work schedules. Allowances are made for wind and tide; in other words certain risks, the key decisions, have been identified. On the voyage there is a continual charting of the course and corrections are made if there is a deviation from the plan. Precisely the same thing should happen on the project. In the ship example, if the navigational checks are not carried out, it is highly probable the ship will land on the rocks; and so will a project. *Without time to measure, assess and control, there may be no more time.*

Progressing

There are three measures that will bring us the greatest chance of success in progressing and controlling the work. Firstly, we must have an adequate plan; secondly, we must know how to be able to measure progress; and thirdly, we must know how to anticipate problems.

We have already discussed the planning aspect; now we must decide how we are to measure the points of progress along the project path. This is not an easy task, especially in technical projects where, say, the testing of a particular device may only give a partial confidence that the device is working correctly. Time may not permit inexhaustible testing of the device; in fact with some electronic devices it would be virtually impossible to 100 per cent test them, as the time factor would be approaching infinity. If, however, we don't have sufficient confidence that we have reached a certain point in the project progress, then theoretically we must not proceed further. This is where the judgement of the project manager and his team really comes into its own. Very often there will be only partial confidence that a particular milestone has been reached, and yet the need to press on is great. Only judgement and the use of normal decision techniques can give the answer.

The third aspect of progress is to endeavour, by means of good planning, experience and good decisions, to actually anticipate the arrival of new problems. We know there is no such thing as a crystal ball, but, with progress, sufficient knowledge and experience, we can get near to success. The three constituents of progress that we are trying to anticipate are time-scales, costs and performance.

Time-scales

By examining very carefully the critical path and near critical paths of the project, we can learn a lot. By noticing the number of contingent events at any one milestone, we can get a clue as to probable trouble areas. It is fairly evident that the chance of a problem arising increases as more and more items have to be completed at a certain point before another item can start, assuming we are in doubt about the progress of these items.

Costs

We should have a planned budget which we can then measure our costs against. We may well need (in most companies we find this so) both an estimate of committed expenditure and an actual accounting return of expenditure. It is not often that the actual accounts are returned quickly enough, especially in a large company with several locations, and thus a committed amount estimated by the project manager is very useful. It is most important that the costs are measured against the planned progress, as we can read quite wrong meanings into any of the cost conditions. For example, if we are underspent or behind-hand with progress, the actual cost is likely to be lower than anticipated, and so we should actually spend money to try and get our progress right if this seems sensible. On the other hand, if we are overspent and progress is ahead of schedule, this may not necessarily be a bad thing, unless our cash flow position is affected too adversely.

Performance

Progress must be measured against performance of parts or units or large end items, and we must try to measure the success at these various milestones. It is rare to find the position quite clear; a judgement will have to be made as to whether to proceed further.

Progress/cost relationship

In some way we must measure progress against expenditure on the task. While completion of a project in a specified time is one of our

224

most essential objectives, we cannot do this regardless of costs. Equally, it is little use underspending and thinking this is a virtue if in fact the project is running late. The main problem in relating progress to cost is that actual cost is clearly and easily measurable, while progress is not so obviously quantifiable. There are two approaches to the problem. One is to split up the project tasks by time and cost, such that one can say: When I have achieved this task, or sub-task, I have achieved, say, £10,000 worth of progress. If this is done throughout the project, it is then possible to relate actual expenditure (real money) to the project achievement in the money terms we have allocated. It does not have to be money which we use as a measure of progress, it could be simply units of progress.

In Figure 15 we have a typical budget/expenditure curve with time as the x axis. Apart from the vagaries of accounting, we should finish up with two curves, one for budget, one for actual expenditure. However, as we have already pointed out, this does not give us any clue about the relationship to progress. If we now, as in Figure 16, have a similar curve, but with the x axis showing progress units or progress money packages, then at any time we can draw a vertical line representing progress in units or money packages, and show the relationship between this and the actual cost. This attempts to put the relationship in quantitative terms. From the picture emerging, one can make a judgement as to the effectiveness of the project. The problem under these conditions is that in most projects the work packages from which the units or money packages have been derived do not stay as neatly bundled as one would like. However, as long as our assessment of budget against work packages is done first, and the actual expenditure and the line marking progress is put in afterwards, the measure can still be obtained.

The second method of relating costs and progress is merely to register progress on, say, a bar chart, register budget and expenditure on another chart and compare the two. The important item in each case is the accurate measurement of progress. Figure 17 shows a typical error in bar charting, where a number of activities are listed, a vertical line is drawn as being the time of review of progress, and the assumption is made that the items on the left of the line are completed. You may well say that this is so simple that surely nobody would fall into such a trap. We have seen many such examples. Figure 18 is one method of doing it

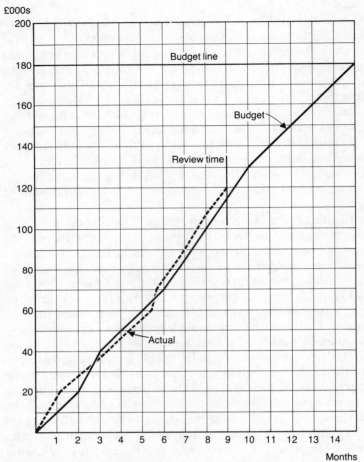

Figure 15   Typical budget/expenditure curve 1

correctly, where the work packages are represented by open rectangles, the review line is again inserted, and on each item the progress is marked by blacking in the rectangle. In Figure 18, therefore, you can see that the first three items are stated to be complete, while the fourth and fifth items are not yet complete, and item 6 is not yet started. This method of marking gives us a fair measure of work done. A further method of indicating the progress on the bar chart is shown in Figure 18, where extensions are shown

226

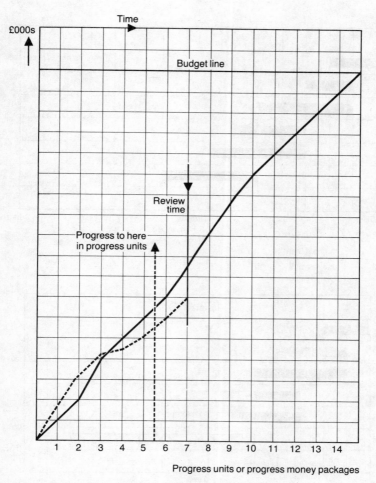

Figure 16 Typical budget/expenditure curve 2

as extra hatched lines on the item to the point where it is estimated it will finish, as shown again on items 4, 5 and 6. The problem in each of these cases is to show clearly whether the item is started or not.

We do not think it appropriate in this book to go into any more detail on this particular point, but the object is to make us all aware of the problem of cost and progress relationships, which is a key area of project management.

227

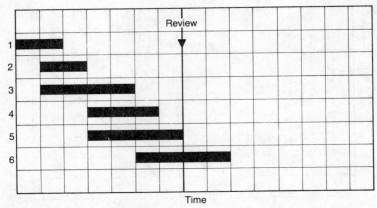

Figure 17   Bar chart 1

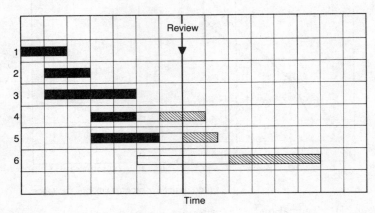

Figure 18   Bar chart 2

Changes

One of the worst offenders in upsetting progress and one which we must control carefully is change. This affects the three items we have discussed, and a rigid change control system should be adopted from the start. In looking at changes we must pay particular attention to those which affect the base lines of the project. These are:

Performance
Specification
Costs
Delivery
Safety
Interfacing
Reliability
Maintainability

There will be others which will not have such a major effect. All changes have to be weighed in the light of both economic and general performance, and a system to evaluate, review and control changes is essential. Firstly there will be a change request for a particular change. Unless the nature of the change is so obvious as to occasion immediate rejection, which is rare, the change control body alerts all interested parties to the change and all comments are reviewed. If this does not cause rejection at this stage, the change must be written by the appropriate body in the form of a detailed proposal, so that, unless it is rejected after this, it is in a form whereby it could be implemented. If it is to be implemented, the change control body must not only see that this is done through the proper channels, but also get a feedback from, say, manufacturing and field operations to support the original decisions.

The change control body may be a permanent feature of the company or it may be set up by the project office. The precise rules for whether or not a change is to be implemented in a particular project are of a tactical nature; they could not therefore be detailed here. However, general rules can be listed:

- *Omission from the original specification of the project.* This has two connotations: can it be done in technical and time-scale terms? Who is going to pay? If it is technically feasible, and the customer will pay, in time (if necessary), and money, then the change may go through.
- *Omission to meet the specification.* Similar to the above, except that the contractor may have to pay. There may be more than one solution with different cost and time penalties.
- *Improvements to the specification.* These require very careful consideration. They may be similar to the omissions, or they may be on that road to perfection, the end of which, of course, we never reach.

229

22 Seven keys to success

We believe that there are seven keys to success as a manager. If you neglect any one of them your chances of success will be impaired. Use all seven and you will develop your full potential as a manager. The seven keys are:

1 Communicate
2 Delegate
3 Control your time
4 Cherish your customers
5 Never stop learning
6 Recognize that knowledge is power
7 Create your own opportunities

We have written about all seven keys in different ways throughout the book. Now let us take a final brief look at each of the keys and how they interact.

Communicate

You have your own objectives. You know your own thoughts and plans. You will only turn these into constructive action if you can communicate them to your staff, your own manager, and all the other people whose co-operation and help is necessary. Telling people what you want is important, but communicating with them is much more than talking at them. As any advertising man will tell you, speech is only one form of communication – a picture is worth a thousand words. Watch John Cleese at work in one of his training films and see how effectively he puts his message across. Communication is two-way. It is essential to watch for the reaction of the people to whom you talk. You must listen to other people. If in any conversation you spend less than half your time listening, you are probably missing something, and it may be important.

Some of the most effective managers we know say very little. They listen carefully. When these managers do speak everyone listens to them and takes note.

Delegate

No manager can do it all alone. He has to work through others. You are likely to get the best results from the people who work for you if you delegate to them. Agree clear objectives with them and then let them work out for themselves how to achieve those objectives. This does not mean that you abdicate your responsibilities. You will want to see and agree their plans. You will want regular reports of progress against plans, and you will be available to listen to your people's problems and to provide advice and guidance when necessary.

Delegation also means that you must be prepared to let your people make mistakes. You must be prepared to accept responsibility for those mistakes yourself. This is hard on you, but your staff will never develop if you do not give them responsibility. They will not learn unless they make some mistakes of their own. At the same time you need to prevent them making really damaging mistakes.

We believe that the way to do this is to agree achievable objectives; require the presentation of a sound plan; discuss the plan; and require regular progress reports.

In discussing the plan and progress, ask questions and let your staff find the weaknesses themselves as they search for the answers. This is much better than uttering dogmatic statements or providing a constant stream of criticism and instruction. Good communication skills are essential if you are to delegate successfully. So long as you retain control, the more you can delegate the better. If your people are capable of doing the job, delegate it to them. You don't keep a dog and bark yourself.

Control your time

The amount of time in the day and in your life is finite. You cannot afford to fritter it away on unimportant things. You must pay heed to the '80:20 rule'. Devote 80 per cent of your time to the work which is critical to success; which is critical to your future; and which only you can do. Less important work must be delegated.

231

The time you devote to routine must be reduced to a minimum.

Control your working day so that you can devote substantial periods to the important aspects of your job without interruptions. Try to set aside at least one hour a day when you can work undisturbed – if necessary the hour before other people reach the office. Set aside half days or even whole days for strategic thinking and planning. In the process of controlling your time, make sure that you do not cut yourself off from your staff or your customers. You must always have time to listen to them.

You are unlikely to maintain control over your time unless you have first learned to delegate to your staff and to communicate effectively with them.

Cherish your customers

It is not just sales and marketing managers who have customers. Every manager has customers, even though they may be people within his own firm or organization. It is the demand of your customers for the goods or services that you supply which keeps you in a job. Make sure that you identify your customers correctly. Then take time and trouble to understand their needs. Establish links with them in good times that will enable you to weather stormy times without going under.

Devote time to improving your knowledge of your customers. Make sure that you know what is important to them. What are the key matters to which they devote their time and thought? What are the key factors in their success? Your understanding of these factors will help you to establish your power base.

If a customer knows you, believes that you understand his needs, and believes that you are trying to help him, then he is likely to be helpful and understanding over your problems. This does not mean that he will be soft with you or accept poor service or faulty goods. He may, however, help you by giving you time to overcome problems. In a market economy the customers and potential customers are the key to a firm's success. While a lot of attention is given to acquiring new customers, it is important to retain your existing ones. Never take them for granted. There are other people in the market-place who will use every opportunity to seduce your customers away from you. Your customers are your most valuable asset. Cherish them.

Never stop learning

You are never too old to learn. No manager can afford to stop learning. Too many people believe that they have learned it all by the time that they leave school or university, or when they pass their professional exams. They expect to coast on through life on what they have learned by their mid-twenties. This may have been possible in the past, though it has never been a reliable recipe for success. Today the pace of change is too fast. Stop learning and you will very quickly become obsolete.

Learning is not all book learning. A great deal can be learned on the job. Learn from doing the job – from your failures and from your successes. Learn by studying your boss and your colleagues. Learn by analysing the successes and the failures of your competitors and of your own firm. But learning is more than this. A great deal of success follows from looking at problems and opportunities from a new perspective. De Bono describes this as lateral thinking. It can be developed by taking experience from one field and transposing it to your own.

Learning requires time. It requires time in significant undisturbed chunks. Learning also involves strong communication skills, both in learning itself and in putting your learning to effective use. Getting people to adopt new or unusual ideas is one of life's most difficult tasks. It requires the highest levels of communication skills.

You can learn to meet the requirements of the next job up the ladder. Identify the likely requirements and start to learn, so that you will be seen to be well equipped for promotion, and so that you will have a flying start when you are promoted.

Knowledge is power

Knowledge is of two kinds. First there is the kind that you have in your own memory, much of it derived from job skill and experience, ready for instant recall and use. The second kind is the knowledge of where to find the answers. The good company secretary may not know all the answers, but he does know where to look up the relevant statutes and case law. When some unusual point of law arises, he knows who is the expert in the field from whom he can obtain advice.

Knowledge is the result of learning. The manager constantly

reviews the knowledge that he needs and sets out to acquire it. The successful manager is concerned not just with the knowledge that he needs tomorrow, but with what he will need to know in three to five years' time.

The basis of the manager's power is his thorough knowledge of his own job. The greater his knowledge of his boss's job and those of his colleagues, the greater his power. The greater his knowledge of his own company and the competition, the greater his power. Study the senior managers in your own company and see which of them really understands the company and its figures. That is where the power lies – and it often lies with the accountant who can understand the realities behind the figures. In the age of information technology more and better information is available to the manager. Be sure that you understand it and know how to use it. If you are using computer-based models and expert systems, it is important to understand the assumptions on which they are based. Don't just accept their results blindly. In a market-led economy, your knowledge and understanding of the market is of supreme importance.

Create your own opportunities

It was several centuries ago that Francis Bacon observed that a wise man will make more opportunities than he finds. Today's manager lives in a competitive world. If he waits for opportunities to find him, he is likely to wait for a very long time. The manager on the way up must set about creating his or her own opportunities.

The creation of opportunities is usually based on a thorough knowledge of the business and a particular problem area. To this is added time spent on careful analysis and a fresh perspective.

Develop an enquiring mind. Constantly ask yourself 'Why?'; 'What if ...?', 'How could we ...?'. Opportunities often arise from successfully using that key communication art – listening. Listening to a customer, a government official or a colleague may reveal to you that the real obstacle to a particular course of action is not the obvious one. That perception provides your opportunity.

Management is not just a science, it is also a creative art. The manager who creates his own opportunities is well on the road to success.

Conclusion

We have described what we believe are the seven keys to success in management. We have shown how these keys are dependent on each other. They are like a kit of parts or the pieces of a jigsaw which combine to make a whole: the final 'key' to success.

No doubt everyone who reads this book could think of some other aspect of management which he or she considers could have been included here. We believe there is one other characteristic which, while not directly contributing to effective management, is possessed by most successful managers. This is their quest for material reward. Make sure that your efforts are recognized and rewarded. You may have, and probably will have, to share your rewards with others. Some people are satisfied that a job well done is reward in itself. If you wish to succeed in management, you will have to take a tougher approach. This is a field in which you have to create your opportunities. As you go up the management ladder, you should be able to negotiate your rewards up-front so that they are linked to your performance. Make sure that your negotiations include what happens if takeovers and the like disrupt your job at that company. Some wise managers have become rich in the process. Recognize your true worth and see that your reward is commensurate with that worth.

Reading list

Part 1

Drucker, P., *Managing in Turbulent Times*, Pan 1981
Hicks, H.G., *The Management of Organisations: A Systems and Human Resources Approach*, 4th ed., McGraw-Hill 1981
Hubbard, B. (ed.), *State of the Art Report: Technology Management*, Series 10, no. 8, Pergamon Infotech 1982
Kotler, P., *Marketing Management*, 5th ed., Prentice Hall 1984
Laurie, P., *The Micro Revolution*, Futura 1980
McCarthy, E.J., *Basic Marketing*, 7th ed., Richard D. Irwin 1981
Toffler, A., *The Third Wave*, Pan 1981

Part 2

Kennedy, G., *Everything is Negotiable: How to Negotiate and Win*, Arrow Books 1984
Kennedy, G., Benson, J., and McMillan, J., *Managing Negotiations*, 2nd ed., Business Books 1984
Melhuish, A., *Executive Health*, Business Books 1978

Part 3

Dixon, N.F., *On the Psychology of Military Incompetence*, Futura 1979
Drucker, P., *The Effective Executive*, Pan 1970
Pascale, R.T. and Athos, A.G., *The Art of Japanese Management*, Penguin 1982
Peter, L.J., and Hull, R., *The Peter Principle*, Pan 1970
Townsend, R., *Up the Organisation*, Coronet 1971

Part 4

Beckett, D.W., *Spicer and Pegler's Book-keeping and Accounts*, H.F.L. Publishers 1980

Clark, P., *Using Statistics in Business*, Pan 1982

Gibbs, J., *A Practical Approach to Management Accounting*, H.F.L. Publishers 1979

Gibbs, J., *A Practical Approach to Financial Management*, H.F.L. Publishers 1980

Holmes, G., and Sugden, A., *Interpreting Company Reports and Accounts*, 2nd ed., Woodhead-Faulkner 1982

Merrett A.J., and Sykes, A., *Capital Budgeting and Company Finance*, Longmans Green & Co 1966

Watling, T.F., and Morley, J., *Successful Commodity Futures Trading*, 2nd ed., Business Books 1978

Part 5

Finch, F., *A Concise Dictionary of Management Techniques*, Heinemann 1976

Harris, H., and Chauhan, E., *So You Want to Buy a Word Processor?*, Business Books 1982

Simons, G.L., *Privacy in the Computer Age*, NCC Publications 1982

Sterling, I.A.L., *The Data Protection Act 1984: A Guide to the New Legislation*, CCH Editions 1984

Taylor, W.J., and Watling, T.F., *Practical Project Management*, Business Books 1973

Taylor, W.J., and Watling, T.F., *Successful Project Management*, 2nd ed., Business Books 1979

Part 6

Watling, Tom, *Plan for Promotion*, Business Books 1977

Index